T0319136

Cambridge Elements ≡

Elements in Public Economics
edited by
Robin Boadway
Queen's University
Frank A. Cowell
The London School of Economics and Political Science
Massimo Florio
University of Milan

EMPIRICAL FISCAL FEDERALISM

Federico Revelli
University of Turin

Emanuele Bracco
University of Verona

CAMBRIDGE
UNIVERSITY PRESS

CAMBRIDGE
UNIVERSITY PRESS

University Printing House, Cambridge CB2 8BS, United Kingdom

One Liberty Plaza, 20th Floor, New York, NY 10006, USA

477 Williamstown Road, Port Melbourne, VIC 3207, Australia

314–321, 3rd Floor, Plot 3, Splendor Forum, Jasola District Centre, New Delhi – 110025, India

79 Anson Road, #06–04/06, Singapore 079906

Cambridge University Press is part of the University of Cambridge.

It furthers the University's mission by disseminating knowledge in the pursuit of education, learning, and research at the highest international levels of excellence.

www.cambridge.org
Information on this title: www.cambridge.org/9781108927000
DOI: 10.1017/9781108918039

First published 2020

A catalogue record for this publication is available from the British Library.

ISBN 978-1-108-92700-0 Paperback
ISSN 2516-2276 (online)
ISSN 2516-2268 (print)

Empirical Fiscal Federalism

Elements in Public Economics

DOI: 10.1017/9781108918039
First published online: October 2020

Federico Revelli
University of Turin

Emanuele Bracco
University of Verona

Author for correspondence: Federico Revelli, federico.revelli@unito.it

Abstract: Fiscal federalism has long been an important topic of inquiry in applied public economics, and interest in the functioning of intergovernmental fiscal relationships in multi-tiered public sector structures does not seem to be fading. Rather, the recent economic downturn and sovereign debt crisis have brought the analysis of multilevel fiscal governance to the forefront of academic discourse and stimulated the search for tax assignments that ease the coordination between authorities at different tiers while preserving local fiscal autonomy and minimizing the harmful effects of taxation on the prospects of economic recovery. This Element examines the recent empirical work in this area and discusses the most critical issues that future research will need to address in order to push further the frontier of econometric analysis in fiscal federalism.

Keywords: fiscal decentralization, political accountability, fiscal competition

ISBNs: 9781108927000 (PB), 9781108918039 (OC)
ISSNs: 2516-2276 (online), 2516-2268 (print)

Contents

1 Introduction

Fiscal federalism has been an important field of inquiry in the public economics literature since Oates's (1972) founding contribution. Understanding the properties and predicting the consequences of alternative arrangements of intergovernmental fiscal relationships in multi-tiered public sector structures on matters such as economic/growth, allocation of resources, political agency relationships, and social welfare is still a hot topic of academic research. Moreover, the sovereign debt crisis of the past decade and the enduring economic downturn have brought the analysis of multi-level fiscal governance to the forefront of academic discourse.

Indeed, federal and unitary countries alike typically share multi-level public finance structures where subcentral government units have an independent role in taxation and public service provision. According to the OECD/UCLG's (2016) investigation of the organizational and financial structure of 101 federal (17) and unitary (84) countries worldwide, comprising more than 500,000 subnational governments and representing almost 6 billion inhabitants, subnational governments account for around one quarter of total government spending or 9% of GDP. In fact, remarkable differences exist between federal and unitary countries. In the former, the share of subnational spending (almost 50% of total public expenditures and 18% of GDP) is more than twice as high as in unitary countries.

The bulk of subnational spending is on education, social protection, public transportation, housing, and community amenities, though the diversity in the assignment of responsibilities across levels of government is enormous. Subnational governments tend to play an important role in public investment, particularly in federal countries, and as public employers, with staff expenditure being their top budget item. Subnational own tax revenues account for about one-fourth of total public revenues and 8% of GDP and are about twice as high in federal as in unitary countries.

Intergovernmental grants play a crucial role in equalization and redistribution. The respective importance of own revenue sources versus transferred ones from other levels of government varies significantly both across countries and over time, as does the degree of regulation, capping, and of various forms of limitations that higher levels of government impose onto lower ones (Revelli, 2016b). The overall combination of those aspects of the fiscal federalism structure of a country determines in the end the degree of financial autonomy of governmental units at each of the existing tiers. In addition, equalization grants that fully or partially compensate local tax base differences (a common feature of federal and unitary countries) tend to influence the own taxation incentives of decentralized policy makers by lowering their marginal cost of raising funds, thus also playing a role in allocative efficiency (Bucovetsky and Smart, 2006; Buettner, 2006; Smart, 2007).

Indeed, the characteristics of multi-tiered fiscal arrangements change over time in response to the evolution of the underlying economic, political, and social structures. In particular, the past decades have seen a trend toward greater decentralization around the globe (Allain-Dupré, 2018). Even though this "silent revolution" (Ivanyna and Shah, 2014) has occurred in almost all regions of the world, the process started earlier in the Western countries, notably in Europe (1960s and 1970s), than in the rest of the world (in Asia and Latin America during the 1990s). In fact, the decentralization revolution seems to have come to a stop in the advanced economies in the most recent years, with a number of unitary countries experiencing a trend of recentralization. Tables 1 and 2 report two basic indicators of public expenditure and revenue decentralization across a number of federal and unitary OECD countries in 1996, in what can be considered the peak of the great decentralization wave, in 2006, right before the beginning of the crisis, and in 2016, almost a decade after the start of the economic recession.

Tables 1 and 2 show that the role of subcentral units is considerable, and even larger than central ones in a number of cases, thus rightly deserving the great deal of attention that they have attracted in the past decades, both theoretically and empirically. However, while subcentral authorities maintain an important function both as revenue-raising bodies and as providers of public services around the developed world, there is no sign of a continuing process of decentralization either on the spending or on the revenue side.

By comparing Tables 1 and 2, it clearly emerges that the share of subcentral governments' expenditures remains consistently larger than the corresponding share of revenues. This constitutes a "vertical fiscal gap" – that is, an excess of local expenditure needs over revenue-raising capacity usually due to a tax assignment that is biased toward the central levels of government as collectors of taxes and that justifies most of the existing top-down intergovernmental transfers. Table 3 reports the subcentral vertical fiscal gap for the years 1996, 2006, and 2016. Overall, the vertical fiscal gap is about 5% to 6% of GDP and shows a large variance between countries, ranging from close to zero to almost 20% of GDP.

Moreover, there is no clear evidence of the vertical fiscal gap being absorbed during those 20 years. This suggests that the search for own revenue sources that can best be attributed to decentralized government units remains at the top of the research agenda in fiscal federalism. At the same time, grants from higher to lower levels of government are likely to

Table 1 Expenditure decentralization (% total government expenditure)

Country		1996	2006	2016
Federal				
Austria	Central	68.24	69.61	68.46
	State-local	31.76	30.39	31.54
Belgium	Central	66.76	61.60	55.13
	State-local	33.24	38.40	44.87
Canada	Central	39.86	33.95	31.85
	State-local	60.14	66.05	68.15
Germany	Central	62.56	62.08	59.91
	State-local	37.44	37.92	40.09
Switzerland	Central	45.63	44.49	42.58
	State-local	54.37	55.51	57.42
United States	Central	52.44	49.91	51.64
	State-local	47.56	50.09	48.36
Unitary				
Czech Republic	Central	65.90	70.52	74.27
	Regional-local	34.10	29.48	25.73
Denmark	Central	46.28	37.09	36.56
	Regional-local	53.72	62.91	63.44
Estonia	Central	74.39	72.65	76.96
	Regional-local	25.61	27.35	23.04
Finland	Central	68.21	61.26	60.69
	Regional-local	31.79	38.74	39.31
France	Central	82.39	80.07	80.60
	Regional-local	17.61	19.93	19.40
Greece	Central	93.20	92.67	92.92
	Regional-local	6.80	7.33	7.08
Hungary	Central	76.16	75.57	87.29
	Regional-local	23.84	24.43	12.71
Ireland	Central	68.24	81.09	92.43
	Regional-local	31.76	18.91	7.57
Israel	Central	87.17	89.01	87.47
	Regional-local	12.83	10.99	12.53
Italy	Central	75.47	69.02	72.52
	Regional-local	24.53	30.98	27.48
Latvia	Central	77.56	72.74	74.59
	Regional-local	22.45	27.26	25.41
Netherland	Central	66.89	67.02	68.62
	Regional-local	33.11	32.98	31.38

Table 1 (cont.)

Country		1996	2006	2016
Norway	Central	64.32	70.10	66.99
	Regional-local	35.68	29.90	33.01
Portugal	Central	87.31	85.73	87.60
	Regional-local	12.69	14.27	12.40
Slovak Republic	Central	89.04	83.31	84.24
	Regional-local	10.96	16.69	15.76
Slovenia	Central	82.88	80.80	81.95
	Regional-local	17.12	19.20	18.05
Spain	Central	65.54	51.01	56.59
	Regional-local	34.46	48.99	43.41
Sweden	Central	62.03	55.37	49.88
	Regional-local	37.97	44.63	50.12
United Kingdom	Central	73.28	71.31	75.89
	Regional-local	26.72	28.69	24.11

Note: Own calculations are based on OECD data.

keep on playing a major role in multi-tiered fiscal structures in the future too, thus justifying the continued interest of empirical public economists in their design and distributional impact, and in the analysis of their effects on local taxation and spending decisions.

In fact, having lagged behind the theoretical literature for decades, empirical research on fiscal federalism issues has been catching up by acquiring a central and independent role in policy advice, formation, and evaluation. This phenomenon is due, on the one hand, to the increasing availability of massive data sets on central and noncentral budgetary items from unitary states and federations; on the other hand, there has been in recent years a parallel development of sharp econometric methods. The latter rely on a clear definition of research questions and smart strategies for identification of key causal effects, thus promising to address the key issues in empirical fiscal federalism research far more successfully and convincingly.

Future research will need to thoroughly examine recent empirical work in this vein and explore the most critical issues in order to expand the frontier of econometric analysis in fiscal federalism, to which this Element is devoted. Given that the volume of empirical contributions in this area is enormous, we will focus on the most recent approaches and contributions.

This Element is structured into two parts. The first part (sections 2–4) covers the classic core endeavors and focuses on three areas of research that have attracted a great deal of scholarly attention in the past decades and can be

Table 2 Revenue decentralization (% total government revenue)

Country		1996	2006	2016
Federal				
Austria	Central	86.42	90.09	89.97
	State-local	13.58	9.91	10.03
Belgium	Central	85.77	82.32	76.42
	State-local	14.23	17.68	23.58
Canada	Central	45.85	45.34	43.62
	State-local	54.15	54.66	56.38
Germany	Central	66.13	64.83	63.18
	State-local	33.87	35.17	36.82
Switzerland	Central	51.22	51.48	51.27
	State-local	48.78	48.52	48.73
United States	Central	58.13	56.55	57.60
	State-local	41.87	43.45	42.40
Unitary				
Czech Republic	Central	82.97	81.94	81.79
	Regional-local	17.03	18.06	18.21
Denmark	Central	68.29	68.44	72.19
	Regional-local	31.71	31.56	27.81
Estonia	Central	96.16	95.60	95.95
	Regional-local	3.85	4.40	4.05
Finland	Central	73.86	74.51	71.74
	Regional-local	26.14	25.49	28.26
France	Central	86.06	84.83	83.99
	Regional-local	13.94	15.17	16.01
Greece	Central	97.34	97.42	97.03
	Regional-local	2.66	2.58	2.97
Hungary	Central	89.03	85.51	92.79
	Regional-local	10.97	14.49	7.21
Ireland	Central	90.38	91.86	95.41
	Regional-local	9.62	8.14	4.59
Israel	Central	92.10	91.78	91.09
	Regional-local	7.90	8.22	8.91
Italy	Central	88.36	81.04	82.67
	Regional-local	11.64	18.96	17.33
Latvia	Central	76.81	81.05	81.83
	Regional-local	23.19	18.95	18.17
Netherland	Central	88.38	89.68	91.22
	Regional-local	11.62	10.32	8.78

Table 2 (cont.)

Country		1996	2006	2016
Norway	Central	80.21	86.84	83.32
	Regional-local	19.79	13.16	16.68
Portugal	Central	90.68	89.69	89.70
	Regional-local	9.32	10.31	10.30
Slovak Republic	Central	94.02	95.04	94.85
	Regional-local	5.98	4.96	5.15
Slovenia	Central	88.81	89.46	88.04
	Regional-local	11.19	10.54	11.96
Spain	Central	82.73	74.20	72.19
	Regional-local	17.27	25.80	27.81
Sweden	Central	67.17	65.77	66.74
	Regional-local	32.83	34.23	33.26
United Kingdom	Central	91.83	90.67	91.45
	Regional-local	8.17	9.33	8.55

Note: Own calculations are based on OECD data.

viewed as the founding pillars of fiscal federalism. In particular, we will first investigate the impact of unconditional grants on recipient governments' spending and fiscal effort, focusing on the anomalous response to grants known as the "flypaper effect." Beyond this, we will turn to the key issue of fiscal externalities due to the mobility of the tax base and the resulting tax competition among same-tier authorities (horizontal fiscal competition). Finally, we will tackle the issue of fiscal externalities among taxing authorities at different levels (vertical fiscal competition) in a multi-tiered government system. This is a relatively (and undeservedly) understudied topic, considering its theoretical importance and its implications for revenue assignment across tiers of government.

The second part of this Element (sections 5–8) covers recent challenges and new frontiers and will turn to the survey of some novel areas of empirical investigation in fiscal federalism and, in particular, the link between decentralization and political accountability. Within this area of research, we will review four main strands. We will first explore how the existence of decentralized governments (and of large panels of data) allowed researchers to shed light on the effect of particular institutional features and advance the understanding of political institutions independently of decentralization, focusing on the link between term limits and political selection and accountability. We will then turn to the effect of voters' information, media penetration, and social capital on accountability and policy choices. Third, we will explore how localities may be

Table 3 Subcentral fiscal gap

Country	1996	2006	2016
Federal			
Austria	−10,73	−10,58	−11,08
Belgium	−10,59	−10,03	−11,93
Canada	−4,46	−3,51	−5,50
Germany	−2,95	−1,84	−1,14
Switzerland	−2,94	−1,82	−2,82
United States	−3,32	−3,70	−4,35
Mean	*− 5,83*	*− 5,25*	*− 6,14*
Unitary			
Czech Republic	−7,65	−5,12	−2,83
Denmark	−13,55	−14,05	−19,21
Estonia	−8,57	−7,58	−7,73
Finland	−4,27	−5,42	−6,66
France	−2,54	−2,86	−2,46
Greece	−2,13	−2,31	−2,04
Hungary	−7,05	−6,46	−2,70
Ireland	−8,68	−3,43	−0,84
Israel	−2,84	−1,40	−1,64
Italy	−7,47	−6,42	−5,46
Latvia	0,17	−3,09	−2,70
Netherlands	−10,30	−9,76	−9,79
Norway	−6,39	−4,46	−7,63
Portugal	−1,90	−2,24	−1,16
Slovak Republic	−3,22	−4,73	−4,52
Slovenia	−2,73	−3,96	−2,97
Spain	−8,32	−8,34	−7,86
Sweden	−4,23	−4,56	−7,96
United Kingdom	−7,23	−8,20	−6,74
Mean	*− 5,73*	*− 5,49*	*− 5,42*

Note: Subcentral fiscal gap = (Subcentral revenues − Subcentral expenditures) as a percentage of GDP; own calculations are based on OECD data.

subject to soft budget constraints and discuss the difficulties in detecting and measuring the effect of local governments expecting to be bailed out by central government in case of financial troubles. Fourth, the last theme in this Element is possibly the central question in the studies of decentralization and fiscal federalism: what evidence there is on the effects of decentralization per se on local government efficiency and public good provision. We will review articles developing cross-country analyses and trying to detect whether political and fiscal decentralization are related in a causal fashion to better (or worse) government outcomes, such as the pervasiveness of corruption.

Finally, the empirical fiscal federalism literature has grown so much in the past decades that reasons of space have forced us to select a limited number of key topics out of a larger number of related important debates of which we provide, where possible, references to up-to-date reviews.

2 The Flypaper Effect

As documented in the introductory section, in virtually all multi-level structures of government, a vertical fiscal gap arises from the widely recognized advantages of assigning the power to tax at the higher tiers and attributing important tasks in the provision of public services to the lower tiers. Indeed, the gap between where tax revenues are collected and where public expenditures are made means that most decentralized authorities throughout fiscal federations will be unable to fund their outlays with their own revenue sources, requiring upper levels of government to intervene to fill the local revenue-expenditure gap with top-down transfers. Intergovernmental grants take many forms and serve different purposes, from unconditional transfers applying to broad categories of spending and leaving beneficiaries with an ample degree of discretion on their use, to grants that are conditional on grantees' programs having clearly defined objectives and satisfying specified conditions (Boadway, 2015).

Here we focus on the popular area of empirical research in fiscal federalism concerning the analysis of the impact of grants from upper-level authorities on lower-level recipient authorities' own expenditures on public services.[1] This line of research amounts to a veritable mountain of thousands of scholarly contributions (more than 3,500 according to Inman's 2009 decade-old count), frequently offering empirical evidence that appears to violate the axioms of microeconomic theory by showing differential responses of local spending to "external" versus "internal" revenue sources (Hines and Thaler, 1995).

To see why this is the case, consider an extremely simple fiscal decentralization arrangement in a two-tiered structure of government, where the expenditures of lower-tier authorities are funded by lump-sum grants from the upper level of government and by nondistortionary revenue sources. Let the welfare W_n of lower-tier jurisdiction $n(n = 1, \ldots, N)$ be expressed as a separable,

---

[1] Gamkhar and Shah (2007) and Sorens (2016) offer deep reviews of the research on the impact of vertical fiscal gaps and equalization grants on local economic performance, rent seeking, and moral hazard in fiscal policy making.

concave function of consumption of pure Samuelsonian public goods and private consumption goods:

$$W_n = v(Z_n) + \rho_n u(c_n) = \ln(Z_n) + \rho_n \ln[i_n(1-\tau_n)], \tag{1}$$

where Z_n stands for total expenditure on local public goods, i_n is the median income in the community, and ρ_n is a positive parameter reflecting the median voter's preferences for private consumption versus consumption of local public goods in locality n. It is assumed that the local authority can raise its own revenues by taxing the community's income at the proportional tax rate τ_n. Assume further that each local authority must abide by a balanced budget rule:

$$Z_n = G_n + \tau_n I_n = G_n + \tau_n \int i_x f(x) d(x), \tag{2}$$

where G_n represents the total lump-sum unconditional grants from the upper tier of the government, I_n is the total taxable income of the community, and $f(x)$ is the density of the income distribution.

Maximization of the welfare function (1) subject to the budget constraint (2) leads jurisdiction n to select the optimal tax rate-spending vector $[\tau_n{}^*, Z_n{}^*]$ as a function of the assumed exogenous variables G_n and I_n:

$$\tau_n^* = [1/(1+\rho_n)] \times [1-\rho_n(G_n/I_n)], \tag{3}$$

$$Z_n^* = [1/(1+\rho_n)] \times (G_n + I_n). \tag{4}$$

Equation (4) generates the standard result that exogenous perturbations in G_n or I_n should be predicted to have an identical effect on $Z_n{}^*$:

$$\partial Z_n^*/\partial G_n = \partial Z_n^*/\partial I_n = 1/(1+\rho_n). \tag{5}$$

When this does not happen – and in particular if a change in grants, in practice, turns out to provoke a larger reaction in local public spending than a change in "own" resources – a "flypaper effect" is said to exist. This section will focus on the most recent empirical investigations of the phenomenon of the excess sensitivity of local government expenditures to changes in grants relative to what conventional microeconomic theory would predict. For the sake of order, we can group these into four major categories, and we will restrict our attention to the most recent pieces of research in each category for reasons of space.[2]

The first category includes the contributions that portray the origin of the flypaper effect as an *econometric issue* related to a variety of specification and

---

[2] Hines and Thaler (1995), Gamkhar and Shah (2007), and Inman (2009) provide excellent reviews of the earlier contributions.

estimation errors that applied researchers would have kept on making for decades. The second explanation points instead to an oversimplification of the theoretical model of local decision-making – in particular, the properties of the mechanism of local revenue generation – as the cause of the "wrong" prediction of an identical impact on expenditures of transferred and own revenue sources. Clearly, the "econometric failure" argument is turned on its head here: it is not the faulty empirical approach that returns incorrect or biased coefficients, but it is the theoretical prediction of the perfect fungibility of funding sources that is "wrong" and does not find support in empirical research. As such, this approach is generally compatible with the standard neoclassical framework, as long as it still relies on the basic assumptions of agents' rationality, stable preferences, and clearing of all markets. Rather, it can be seen as a refinement of the theory that is obtained by introducing more realistic assumptions on the underlying local fiscal institutions and by allowing local governments to rely on distortionary sources of revenue. The third explanation is based on the recognition that recipient governments are subject to several constraints on their own revenue sources or spending decisions (tax and expenditure limitations) that are formally established by upper levels of government. In such a constrained environment, grant changes might be the only way to modify their levels of expenditures and get closer to their desired public-private consumption mix. Finally, the fourth explanation is qualitatively different from the previous ones, in that it explains the fact that money "sticks where it hits," with an explicit failure of some of the key assumptions of the neoclassical model of rational decision-making. In what follows, we will discuss the evidence that has emerged from those four lines of research, in turn.

2.1 Econometric Issues

The anomalously high response of local public expenditures to changes in grants relative to changes in local private resources might be due to econometric problems. In turn, these can have two distinct origins. The first is an issue of the specification of the local public expenditure equation, related to the characteristics of the grant variable that is included among the explanatory variables. The second econometric problem is more subtle and difficult to solve, even though it is, again, a specification issue, in the sense that it arises from the fact that the magnitude of a grant that flows to a locality may depend on local characteristics (observable or unobservable) that also have an independent impact on expenditure levels. First, any omitted variable that has a direct effect both on local expenditures and on grants – say, adverse climatic conditions, extreme events like flooding or earthquakes, or unobserved preferences for local public goods – will provoke a bias in the estimate of the impact of grants on expenditures. In addition, in several circumstances, the size of grants to a locality will depend on the choices made in the past by the recipient authority, which still influence the current level of expenditures. Finally, as long as grants intend to equalize differences in the cost of providing public services and are therefore based on variables (e.g., age structure of the population, income deprivation, or own fiscal capacity) that have a direct impact on actual levels of local expenditures, obtaining a consistent estimate of the impact of grants on local spending requires that those needs/capacity indicators be related to grants in a different way than they are related to actual expenditures.

The grant endogeneity problem can be addressed in either of the following ways. The first consists in finding appropriate instruments for grants, ideally deriving from a rigorous theoretical model. The second exploits the features of the grant distribution formulas that create nonlinearities or kinks at specified indicators' thresholds, aimed at consistently estimating the impact of grants by functional form considerations or using exogenous changes at those discontinuities. We discuss those two approaches in turn.

i. Theoretically derived instrumental variables. Part of the recent literature has sought an explanation for the flypaper effect in the features of the political federal-state bargaining process underlying the attraction of funding for large public works, searching for instruments that could address the potential endogeneity of federal aid in an equation of determination of recipient state governments' public expenditures on infrastructures. Early influential research by Knight (2002) was based on the idea that both US federal grants and state government spending decisions are frequently determined through a political bargaining process, with the former tending to reflect underlying constituent preferences through their elected representatives in key federal assemblies' committees. In his empirical work, Knight (2002) used a measure of congressional power – namely, the proportion of congressional delegates serving in the US federal transportation authorization committee – as an instrument for federal grants and concluded that there was no flypaper effect once grant endogeneity was properly accounted for. Unlike in OLS (Ordinary Least Squares) estimates, federal funds were estimated to almost fully (about 90 cents per dollar) crowd out state own financial efforts in IV (Instrumental Variables) estimates.

A similar result was found by Dupor (2017), who estimates a crowd-out effect of about 80 cents per dollar using data on highway federal funding to states provided by the 2009 American Recovery and Reinvestment Act (ARRA) – a federal program of an additional $28 billion to the around $50 billion states were spending on highways in 2008, before the ARRA. Several states indeed decreased their total capital spending on highways upon receipt of those grants, freeing their own resources for other uses, with little or no impact on employment in the highway, bridge, and street construction industry. Using the cumulative per capita state highway outlays from before to after the reform as the dependent variable, Dupor (2017) finds virtually no flypaper effect from the ARRA grant, which imposed no requirement on states to match any fraction of highway projects' costs, making those funds fully fungible. Moreover, the grant was strictly formula based and used indicators that were determined several years before the act's passage, thus allowing one to consider the variation in per capita highway aid received by states as exogenous and apply a causal interpretation to the estimated coefficient of grants on state expenditure.

On the other hand, Nesbit and Kreft (2009) and Leduc and Wilson (2017) obtained results that seem at odds with the evidence of almost complete crowd-out in Knight (2002) and Dupor (2017). Nesbit and Kreft (2009) study US state highway spending from 1994 to 2002, a period where state highway programs were largely funded by federal grants and earmarked taxes. The former followed a reimbursement rule, according to which the Federal Highway Administration (FHA) first allocates the grants to the states, then the states "obligate" those funds for specific projects, and finally the FHA distributes the funds after project expenses have been sustained by the states. The latter comes from highway users' taxes and fees. Nesbit and Kreft (2009) set up a two-stage, least-squares approach where in the first stage, federal highway grants paid to a state are regressed on current and lagged state obligations, while in the second stage, state highway expenditures are regressed on the predicted values of grants from the first stage and earmarked revenues, yielding estimates of a one-for-one response of spending to federal grants. However, it seems dubious that state obligations can be taken as valid instruments (wherein the exclusion restrictions are not tested) and that earmarked tax revenues can be assumed to be exogenous. In fact, the estimated coefficients from the second-stage equation seem to reflect the features of a budgetary equilibrium rather than the actual behavioral response of state policy makers to exogenous revenue shocks from either external or internal sources. Leduc and Wilson (2017) study the impact of ARRA highway grants of 2009 with a similar methodology of Dupor (2017). They employ a strong research design based on a difference-in-difference estimator, where the time difference in state highway spending per capita is taken relative to the year before the ARRA funds were distributed (2008), thus removing any time-invariant state influence on the level of spending, to recover the yearly impact of the one-time transfer shock in the subsequent years 2009 to 2013. Unlike Dupor (2017), though, they opt for an IV approach based on the argument that the size of federal aid might be endogenous, for two reasons.

First, states with more intense road-related factors represented in the grant distribution formula might have been hit harder by the recession, thus possibly creating a spurious correlation between ARRA highway grants and state highway spending. Second, part of the ARRA grants might be distributed by the Department of Transportation in an endogenous way, based on political considerations. They use two sets of instrumental variables. The first is made of a subset of the road-related factors used in the 2009 ARRA grant apportionment formula (interstate lane miles and contributions to the Highway Trust Fund) that can be considered exogenous due to long measurement lags. The second set of instruments consists of state highway miles in the original 1944 interstate highway system proposal, which are highly correlated with the contemporary highway structure and predict ARRA highway grants more accurately than instruments based on states' political power in Congress (Knight, 2002). Both OLS and IV estimates using these instruments provide strong evidence of a flypaper effect, with spending in highways reacting on an almost dollar-for-dollar basis to the large temporary increase in federal grants under the 2009 ARRA in the first year after the implementation of the program. Moreover, they find a cumulative effect over the three subsequent years of two to three dollars of extra spending for each dollar of ARRA highway grant, suggesting crowd-in of states' own funding due to the complementarity of federally funded highway infrastructures with state-funded minor connection roads and corridors. Finally, they investigate the role of special interest groups and their contributions to state-office candidates, showing that the latter grew considerably during the 2009/2010 electoral cycle, consistent with the hypothesis that road construction companies lobbied heavily to have their state governments spend the highway funds as intended and not divert them to other uses. When interacting grants received by a state with public works contributions in the highway spending equation, they find some evidence that states with higher shares of political contributions from the public works sector also increased spending on highways as a result of the receipt of the ARRA funds.

In a different institutional context, Bracco et al. (2015) develop a political agency model of a two-tiered structure of government where politicians signal their ability through higher spending on public goods, voters have an ideological preference for either of two parties, and grants from central to local governments are unobserved by voters. In such an environment, the upper-level government distributes grants strategically in order to raise the popularity of lower-level incumbents that are aligned with (i.e., belong to the same party as) the central government. In an empirical work on Italian local government data, Bracco et al. (2015) compare municipalities where the incumbent mayor is barely aligned with the central government (i.e., won the election by a tiny vote margin) and those where the incumbent mayor is barely unaligned, in a regression discontinuity framework. They find that aligned mayors receive more grants and are more likely to be reelected than those who are not aligned with the grant donor. Next, they instrument grants with the political alignment dummy variable, finding that grants still have a large impact on local public expenditures, while private local income has a negligible effect on spending. These two results are in line with the existence of the flypaper effect, as predicted by their model, where the excess sensitivity of spending to grants is the result of the hypotheses they make about residents' preferences and the deadweight loss of local taxation.

Finally, Lutz (2010) examines the impact of a school finance reform in New Hampshire that, following a declaration of the unconstitutionality of property-tax-based systems of funding by the Supreme Court, produced exogenous positive or negative wealth shocks to communities, while leaving them in full control of school finances. He presents the argument that democratic institutions of representation – such as direct versus representative democracy – might be responsible for the degree to which a polity's preferences are actually translated into collective choices. The school finance reform in New Hampshire took place in an institutional setting where most municipalities were characterized by direct decisions of the citizenry regarding public budgets. Moreover, citizens could be assumed to be well informed, and the change in grants due to the reform was large and unpredicted. He found that in such a context of widespread information and civic engagement, the additional education transfers crowded out local education funding almost entirely, causing the flypaper effect to vanish and suggesting that the flypaper effect found in many institutional contexts characterized by representative democracy in fact might be due to misalignment between voters' and decision-makers' preferences.

ii. Grant formula discontinuities. Following the approach of Gordon (2004) and Dahlberg et al. (2008), the issue of endogeneity of grants has been increasingly addressed by exploiting discontinuities in grant distribution formulae. Such discontinuities are frequently due to the existence of thresholds for eligibility to specific components of the transfer, and have the effect of provoking discrete exogenous changes in the number of grants when a conditioning variable crosses the threshold, with those same conditioning variables typically having an independent effect on local expenditures. The fundamental idea behind this approach can be seen as a blend of a standard instrumental variables estimator with the mechanics of the grant distribution formula. Say that the focus of the analysis is to get a point estimate of the impact of a change in total grants (ΔG_{nt}) on the change in local public spending (ΔZ_{nt}) in a first-differenced specification, removing all time-invariant local characteristics, with n indexing local authorities and t time, and $\Delta\varepsilon_{nt}$ being the differenced residual. Say that the change in grants depends on the short-term variation in a vector of variables Δs_{nt}, where it can be the case that $E(\Delta\varepsilon_{nt}|\Delta s_{nt}) \neq 0$, and on the change in a conditioning variable Δp_{nt} relative to a fixed threshold p^*. For instance, a component of the grant might change discretely when p_{nt} happens to exceed the threshold. In addition, p_{nt} might have an independent direct effect on G_{nt}. The idea is to use the formula-driven grant change predicted by the conditioning variable $p_{nt}\left(\Delta G_{nt}^* = G(s_{nt-1}, p_{nt}) - G(s_{nt-1}, p_{nt-1})\right)$ as an instrument for ΔG_{nt} in the first stage, and include a smooth function of the conditioning variable $\varphi(\Delta p_{nt})$ in the second stage equation to allow for a direct continuous effect of that variable on spending.

Lundquist (2015) applies a difference-in-differences approach to the analysis of the impact of grants on expenditures in Finnish municipalities that is based on the existence of a supplemental grant given to remotely populated localities. Local authorities are divided into groups and receive (or do not receive) the supplemental grant based on the value of a remote population index computed by the National Statistics Institute. In addition, a reform implemented in 2002 – in the middle of the data observation period – sharply raised the supplemental grant for eligible authorities. The estimates suggest a sudden, large, and persistent impact of grants on local expenditures – a result that is robust to an alternative identification strategy based on a regression discontinuity design around the treatment cutoff.

Allers and Vermeulen (2016) exploit a reform of the fiscal equalization system in the Netherlands that provoked large changes in grants to local governments to test the hypothesis that the flypaper effect can be caused by "rent-seeking." The idea is that if additional grants are mostly used for nonproductive public spending (rents), then one should observe little or no capitalization of those grants into property values, given that the extent of capitalization reflects the value that the marginal homebuyer attaches to how a marginal increase in grants is spent. The reform they exploit took place in two phases between the late 1990s and the first half of the 2000s, and involved strengthening the equalization component of the grant distribution formula by focusing on a number of needs-related variables over which municipalities had no control. Given that the reform provoked large changes in grants to municipalities, during the move to the new regime, local authorities received temporary negative or positive transition grants to smooth excessive short-term variations. The smoothed changes in grants due to the reform are used as instruments for total grants per capita in an equation of local tax revenue determination, as well as in a hedonic equation where the house price index is used as the dependent variable. The results show that exogenous grant changes had little impact on local residential property tax revenues but were fully capitalized into house prices – a result that is inconsistent with the view that the high sensitivity of spending to grants be caused by rent appropriation by politicians or bureaucrats. The absence of an effect on municipal public employment reinforces the conclusion that the grants were not used to expand the bureaucracy and that the rent-seeking explanation for the observed flypaper effect is unlikely.

In fact, the rent-seeking explanation of the flypaper effect predicts different responses of beneficiaries' own tax-setting behavior to rising and falling grants – a point that is explicitly addressed in a paper by Gennari and Messina (2014). They use panel data on Italian municipalities to test a number of hypotheses concerning the flypaper effect, and in particular, they focus on the asymmetric response of local expenditures to grant increases and grant cuts – an issue that has attracted the attention of empirical researchers in a somewhat sparse way during the past decades (Gamkhar and Oates, 1996). The idea is that allowing for a differential response depending on the sign of the grant variation might reveal the underlying objective function of policy makers. First, there is no reason to expect an asymmetric response of spending to grant cuts and rises if policy makers simply reflect the median voter's preferences and smoothly adjust local taxes accordingly in the absence of further constraints. On the other hand, empirical evidence of local spending reacting on a one-for-one basis to rising grants, with grant cuts being followed instead by local tax rises to almost fully compensate for the loss in external funding (a "replacement effect"), would be compatible with a budget-maximizing hypothesis.[3] To tackle the potential problem of grant endogeneity, Gennari and Messina (2014) first use an IV approach, where lags of grants are used as instruments, and then exploit a discontinuity in the grant distribution formula. They find evidence of a flypaper effect, with the response to grants being 20 to 40 times larger than the response to income. However, the little evidence of an asymmetric response (i.e., lack of replacement of external with internal sources of funding when grants fall) implies that they can ascribe only a little portion of the flypaper effect to misalignment between elected representatives' and voters' preferences for spending on public services.

Finally, Liu and Ma (2016) study the flypaper effect issue in a particular decentralized context like the Chinese one, where local officials are not elected and are therefore not accountable to the citizenry but are appointed by upper-level governments through the Chinese Communist Party. Since those

---

[3] A different sort of asymmetry would arise if a cut in grants were followed by a cut in local taxes too – a "fiscal restraint" effect that would lead to a "super-flypaper effect" (local spending falling more than the grant cut) that would be hard to reconcile with standard microeconomic theory and that has received little empirical support in the literature.

appointed local bureaucrats might aim at maximizing own rewards that are increasing in the size of the budget, this would push toward a large impact of grants on expenditures. On the other hand, interjurisdictional competition for mobile resources might work as an automatic backstop to excessive spending, and while statutory tax rates are uniformly set by central authorities, local governments can alter the effective tax rates through their discretionary power in tax enforcement. By employing a regression discontinuity design approach where rural income per capita (a threshold of which enters the grant distribution formula to identify the National Poor Counties) is used as an instrument for the actual transfers received, they consistently estimate the impact of a discrete change in fiscal transfers on the expenditures of the counties slightly above and below the threshold. They find that the "lack of political accountability" effect prevails: grant increases translate into one-for-one changes in local expend-itures, with virtually no crowding out of own revenues and no evidence of a disciplining effect on the mobility of economic resources.

Overall, the search for econometric approaches that promise to return the most accurate and credible estimates of the impact of grants on local expend-itures by fully exploiting the economic theory as well as the institutions governing the distribution of transfers remains one of the most important, challenging, and promising areas of research in empirical fiscal federalism in an era of fiscal recentralization.

2.2 Income Effects, Price Effects, and the Marginal Cost of Public Funds

A second explanation of the flypaper effect relies on the idea that, in reality, lump-sum grants generate a price effect in addition to the income effect when recipient governments use distortionary taxation to fund local public spending – an early intuition by Hamilton (1986) that has been recently formally exposed by Dahlby (2011). The underlying mechanism is that a lump-sum transfer to a subnational government in principle allows it to reduce the tax rates on the own distortionary sources of revenues and keep on providing the same level of services as it did before the transfer. Say the local government maximizes the welfare V of a homogeneous immobile population, it raises own revenues by setting a tax rate τ on a tax base having a tax rate elasticity ε_τ, and receives lump-sum grants from the central government to provide a local public good g. Optimal spending on the public good must satisfy the equality condition between the marginal benefit of the public good to the representative taxpayer (the ratio of the marginal utility of the public good to the marginal utility of income V_g/V_Y) and the marginal cost of providing it: $MC = c_g \times MCF(\tau, \varepsilon_\tau)$, where c_g is the constant per unit cost of producing g, and the marginal cost of funds MCF satisfies $MCF(\tau, 0) = MCF(0, \varepsilon_\tau) = 1$, $\partial MCF(\tau, \varepsilon_\tau)/\partial \tau > 0$, and $\partial MCF(\tau, \varepsilon_\tau)/\partial \varepsilon_\tau > 0$. This implies that, at the new equilibrium with lower own tax rates, and as long as those revenue sources are indeed distortionary ($\varepsilon_\tau \neq 0$), the marginal cost of funds is lower and so is the effective price of providing public services. Dahlby (2011) shows that the substitution effect of a lump sum grant will be larger in parallel with the ratio of lump-sum grants to the own-source tax revenues collected by the subnational government and, under reasonable assumptions, when the grant-recipient government's marginal cost of funds is higher. Numerical simulations based on plausible values of the key model parameters (marginal utility of income, marginal cost of funds, share of subnational taxes on residents' income, tax base elasticity) suggest that the effect of a lump-sum grant on spending would be up to five times larger than the effect of a local private income increase. Indeed, besides providing a coherent justification of the flypaper effect, the marginal-cost-of-public-funds explanation has an obvious yet powerful implication. As far as federal/central government taxation creates fewer distortions than state/local ones, vertical intergovernmental transfers should be preferred on purely efficiency grounds, rather than on the more conventional intergovernmental equity arguments, to the decentralization of own revenue sources to local governments.

Recently, the marginal-cost-of-public-funds argument has been revived and tested empirically by Aragón (2013) and Dahlby and Ferede (2016). Aragón (2013) focuses on the role of the cost of local tax collection in explaining the high responsiveness of spending to grants. While not representing an excess burden of taxation in a strict sense, tax collection costs play a similar role in the argument and lend themselves easily to empirical implementation because they can be captured by measurable proxies. In particular, Aragón (2013) uses information on the existence of automated collection systems and tax base measurement in Peruvian district municipalities to find that low collection cost authorities adjust their expenditures to grants to a significantly smaller extent (0.5 to 0.7) than high collection cost authorities (0.8 to 1).

Dahlby and Ferede (2016) formalize and test the hypothesis that the impact of intergovernmental grants on expenditures is positively correlated with the marginal cost of public funds of the recipient government. They perform an empirical analysis on Canadian provinces where they proxy the marginal cost of public funds with the elasticity of provincial income tax bases to changes in personal income tax rates. Their specification of the consolidated provincial and local expenditure determination equation includes the proxy for the marginal cost of public funds and its interaction with federal aid to provinces. Two potential problems arise in the estimation of that equation. First, the marginal cost of public funds might be endogenous in the expenditure determination equation because it depends on the income tax rate set by the province. As a result, they use other provinces' income tax rates (weighted by the inverse of the distance between population centers) as instruments for a province's own marginal cost of public funds. Second, the fiscal capacity of a province both affects the magnitude of federal grants it receives, thus indirectly influencing spending, and has a direct impact on provincial spending by determining its ability to generate own revenues. Moreover, given that some of the dimensions of the revenue-raising capacity of a province might be unobserved, grants should be allowed to be endogenous. Dahlby and Ferede (2016) adopt a similar IV approach as Dahlberg et al. (2008) and use as instruments for grants the components of the grant distribution formula that are independent of provincial spending decisions and that create a discontinuity in the allocation of grants. In particular, they exploit the fact that a province is entitled to equalization grants if its own per capita fiscal capacity is below the per capita revenue of the reference group of provinces. Moreover, they control for a smooth function of provincial fiscal capacity in the expenditure determination equation. Their evidence is compatible with a large flypaper effect (a response of spending to grants of around 0.8 and to own private resources of about 0.1) and is weakly supportive of the hypothesis that the stimulative effect of federal grants increases with the provinces' marginal cost of public funds.

Finally, Vegh and Vuletin (2016) use data on Argentinian provinces and Brazilian states to test the main predictions of their model – namely that the size of the flypaper effect is increasing in the level of the recipient governments' tax rate (being the tax distortion increasing in the intensity of the tax effort) and is decreasing in the degree of substitutability between private and public spending. With low elasticity of substitution, government spending is not easily substitutable for private spending, the community has a higher degree of tolerance of tax distortions, and extra transfers will trigger an increase in public spending that is larger than the one following an equivalent gain in income. In fact, the flypaper effect is predicted to vanish with perfect substitutability between public and private consumption goods. In order to test the first implication, they use the Argentinian sample and split it in provinces with above-median and below-median tax rates. Evidence of the flypaper effect arises both in the Argentinian and in the Brazilian sample, with a grant coefficient that is not statistically different from 1. However, they find a flypaper effect of a significantly larger magnitude in the high tax rate Argentinian provinces than in the low tax rate ones. As for the second prediction, they classify spending categories according to the extent they correspond to the "pure public good" paradigm, with high degrees of "publicness" assumed to be associated with low degrees of substitutability between public and private spending. They find a significant flypaper effect for public goods outlays, while there is no evidence of an excess sensitivity to grants for spending categories associated with private goods. In a related paper, Vegh and Vuletin (2015) put forward the novel argument that the differential response of spending to different revenue sources can be rationalized if the sources of revenues (private income and public transfers) are uncertain and imperfectly correlated with one another, and if public resources are less volatile than local private resources. Following this macroeconomic insurance reasoning and under the hypothesis of incomplete markets, an increase in grants will raise the variance of total available resources by less than what an increase in private income would, leading to smaller additional precautionary savings and larger expenditure on public services as a rational response to the change in the composition of funds. Empirically, one should find that the flypaper effect is a decreasing function of the correlation between public and private resources, and the effect of such correlation on the flypaper effect should be increasing in the degree of volatility of those resources. Using data on the provinces of Argentina, Vegh and Vuletin (2015) find supportive evidence of the implications of their theoretical model, though in quantitative terms, the insurance argument can explain only a fraction (about 12%) of the total flypaper effect.

2.3 Institutional Explanations

The theoretical model that is conventionally employed to study local government responses to variations in grants assumes that local governments select the level of public expenditure that maximizes their objective function, be it a measure of local welfare, the utility of the members of their constituency, or the amount of rents they can appropriate. The only constraint to their choices is their budget – say, a balanced budget in every period – leaving them the freedom to pick the feasible tax and expenditure mix that they wish. However, local governments are typically subject to a plethora of rules, obligations, and limitations that prevent them from making the choices that they would make in the absence of those rules, most frequently including explicit top-down tax and expenditure limitations (Revelli, 2016b).

Indeed, incorporating those further constraints into a model of local decision-making is likely to have consequences on the prediction of the way local governments will respond to changes in external sources of revenue. Brooks and Phillips (2010) offer the first formal enunciation and empirical test of the hypothesis that restrictive fiscal institutions might be responsible for the fly-paper effect. They argue that tax and expenditure limitations imposed by the states may have systematically forced city governments to underprovide local public goods and be responsible for the high stimulative effect of federal grants on city spending. In fact, spending all of any additional grant money instead of returning it to taxpayers via lower taxes could in frequent circumstances be the only way for local governments to get closer to the median voter's ideal point. To test that hypothesis, they use data on the US Community Development Block Grant (CDBG) program, one of the largest federal grant schemes to cities that is based on formulas that account for relative deprivation, along with information on fiscal limitations on city budgets. However, since Brooks and Phillips (2010) do not observe whether a revenue-raising constraint is actually binding in any given city, they rely on a state-level index of fiscal constraints and cannot model the endogenous selection of a city government into the fiscally constrained status. Interestingly, Brooks and Phillips (2010) find in general a very high sensitivity of spending to grants, while they find only limited evidence of an effect of statutory state-level tax limitations on municipal governments' response to the collapse in CDBG grants.

Revelli (2013) considers a two-tiered structure of government where the lower level of government raises own revenues from a number of different tax bases and receives unconditional grants from the upper level, and models theoretically the endogenous tax mix determination process by lower-level authorities in the presence of exogenous tax rate limitations imposed by the upper-level authority. He shows how the flypaper effect arises in the endogenously generated constrained tax mix, in the sense that local expenditures display a one-for-one response to grants in the presence of binding limitations on all local tax revenue sources. Revelli (2013) shows theoretically that a binding cap on just one of the available own local revenue sources is sufficient to generate some form of flypaper effect – that is, an excess sensitivity of local public spending to grants. Interestingly, this result holds when either upper or lower tax limitations are binding: local authorities will display an excess sensitivity of public expenditures to grants irrespective of whether they are against lower or upper tax rate limits. By means of an empirical application to panel data on Italian local governments' budgets, where local authorities are subject to strict and frequently binding upper and lower tax rate limitations, Revelli (2013) shows that authorities that are not fully constrained turn out to be able to smooth out their expenditure profile by offsetting state grant policy through own tax changes. On the other hand, there is a one-for-one response of spending to grants in tax-constrained localities, irrespective of whether upper or lower limits bind. An important corollary of Revelli's (2013) analysis concerns the very interpretation of the public-spending behavior that is conventionally known as the flypaper effect. Since excess sensitivity of local public spending to grants is predicted to arise, and generally tends to manifest itself, both when grants increase and when they decrease, the flypaper effect label turns out to be a misleading one. Unlike the commonly held belief that the flypaper effect can be the result of profligate and inefficient policy makers refusing to return grant money to the citizenry via tax cuts, a higher sensitivity of local public expenditures to grants than to own revenue sources cannot, in general, be interpreted as a symptom of decentralized government overspending.

More recently, Goeminne et al. (2017) examine the effects of a temporary fiscal restriction introduced in Belgium in 2008 – a "local fiscal pact" between the central government and Flemish local authorities according to which local authorities cannot either introduce new taxes or raise the rates of the existing ones, and agree to gradually drop some existing ones on business. They estimate an expenditure determination equation on a panel data set of Flemish municipalities crossing the date of the introduction of the fiscal pact, making it possible to estimate the differential impact of grants on local outlays after the reform. First, they find that during the entire period of observation the response of local expenditures to grants is about 0.7, in line with previous results on Flemish municipal data. Second, they find that during the year the fiscal pact is in place, and in the subsequent years, local expenditures respond to a significantly larger extent to grants than during the period preceding it.

In general, and while admitting that collecting accurate information on the tax and expenditure limitations local governments are subject to in different institutional contexts can be an extremely demanding task, overlooking the fact that grant variations can be the only means of getting closer to the desired mix of consumption of public services can lead to unsound and misleading conclusions. Incorporating the fiscal limitations imposed onto local governments both in theoretical and empirical modeling of local decision-making processes can be of crucial importance to understand the reaction of decentralized decision makers to changes in external sources of revenue.

2.4 Behavioral Explanations

Finally, it has been argued that the flypaper effect might be the product of "behavioral phenomena" – that is, of violations of some of the fundamental assumptions of the neoclassical paradigm underlying the traditional decision-making process (Hines and Thaler, 1995). First, it has been argued that the taxpayers of a community might systematically mistake lump-sum aid for matching aid. The large impact of grants on recipient governments' spending would thus arise because voters do not fully understand the complexity of grant programs, in particular by taking lump-sum grants accruing to their local government as affecting (lowering) the price of public services relative to private consumption. This misperception would induce residents to demand more public service because they believe their price to be lowered by the grant (a substitution effect), while no such perception arises if private income increases by the same amount as the grant. The early work in this direction did not provide any compelling evidence in this respect though (Inman, 2009), and the most recent research has virtually abandoned this line of investigation, also due to the difficulties that emerge when empirically implementing these tests (Ryu, 2017).

More fundamentally, it has been argued that even if taxpayers knew the actual (lump-sum) characteristics of the external resources accruing to their local authorities, they might still perceive public resources and private resources as not entirely fungible due to a process of "mental accounting" (Thaler, 1999). Mental accounting refers to the idea that people would let their choices about the allocation of money be influenced by the origin of that money, thus violating the fundamental hypothesis of money fungibility. For example, consumers would tend to spend more out of unexpected, one-time payoffs (refunds, bonuses, wins) than out of regular sources of income. Further, they would treat money from different sources with different degrees of care and prudence, and even formally categorize and record it with different labels, thus creating artificial constraints on the use of what are in reality unique budgets. With reference to decision-making in local public economics, mental accounting would imply that the social marginal utility of public funds is itself dependent on where these funds come from (local taxpayers' pockets or nationwide taxpayers' ones), thus making the selected level of local public services depend on the composition of its sources of funding. The higher (lower) the share of external top-down funding, the higher (lower) the equilibrium level of public services that will be provided, and the higher (lower) the sensitivity of expenditures on local public goods to changes in external funds. In fact, while the behavioral approach to the analysis of decision-making is gaining increasing popularity in general public economics (Alm and Sheffrin, 2017), and in spite of the passionate endorsement made more than 20 years ago by Hines and Thaler (1995), systematic analyses of the flypaper effect in these terms have lagged behind, either with real local government data or with experimental ones.

As far as the latter is concerned, in a recent paper, Becker et al. (2018) test the hypothesis of mental accounting in a laboratory context that recreates the typical collective decision-making dilemmas of multi-level government envir-onments. In particular, they set up a redistribution game where the "rich" players have access to a common pool of resources of variable size that can be used for redistributive purposes. If not, those resources are returned to the "rich" players after each round of the game. Of course, the size of such a "common account" should be entirely irrelevant to rich players' choices unless it is mentally accounted for differently than players' private accounts. Their experiment shows that where the money nominally comes from matters, in the sense that the transfer increases in the relative size of the common account – a result that can be taken as a direct test of the mental accounting hypothesis, given that all other potentially confounding factors (i.e., institutional, or the cost of raising funds) are removed.

There seems to be a strong need for further testing of real as well as laboratory data on the relevance of the mental accounting hypothesis. In particular, it seems worth investigating further to what extent the flypaper effect arises from recipients of grant money labeling and categorizing the money they receive, thus creating *artificial* restrictions on the set of available choices concerning how that money could be spent, and to what extent they are indeed subject to frequently overlooked yet *real* constraints on their choices.

3 Horizontal Fiscal Externalities

The second area of empirical fiscal federalism research that we address concerns the phenomenon of fiscal competition. Fiscal competition can either be horizontal – that is, it involves governments from the same tier that compete with each other to attract mobile resources (tax competition) or to boost their electoral chances by improving their own performance relative to that of comparable governments (yardstick competition; Besley and Case, 1995b) – or vertical, between governments at different tiers. We treat the case of horizontal fiscal competition here and devote section 4 to the analysis of the most recent empirical works on vertical fiscal competition.[4]

Horizontal fiscal competition has attracted a great deal of attention from applied public economists in recent years and has led to widespread adoption of spatial econometric methods whose potential and limits remain to be fully understood (Revelli, 2015a). This section will review the most recent literature tackling the issues that emerge when applying those econometric methods to the analysis of intergovernmental fiscal interactions in federal and unitary countries.

The most recent research in this area has increasingly attempted to exploit quasi-experimental circumstances that generate exogenous variation in the fiscal policies of a set of local authorities in order to identify the impact of those fiscal policy shocks on the behavior of neighboring sets of authorities that

---

[4] The two main waves of the voluminous empirical yardstick competition literature are extensively reviewed in Revelli (2006) and Revelli (2015a), respectively.

are not directly affected by those changes. This setup promises to address in a more credible and convincing way the simultaneity of local governments' decisions and to lead to a consistent estimate of the size and direction of substantive fiscal interactions (Gibbons and Overman, 2012). In fact, many of the papers that have employed this approach have failed to find significant evidence of tax mimicking or strategic fiscal interaction between local authorities, calling into question the straightforward application of the conventional spatial econometric techniques borrowed from geographical analysis to the empirical analysis of fiscal competition.

In the rest of this section, we will first consider the most recent empirical analyses of tax competition that explicitly tackle the estimation of a spatial tax reaction function. Next, we will highlight the key econometric issues that emerge when trying to estimate the impact of local taxation on households "voting with their feet" – that is, migrating to the localities offering the desired bundle of public goods and taxes. We will focus, in particular, on the border-discontinuity approaches that have been employed to address the tax policy endogeneity issues that typically arise in empirical work estimating the elasticity of the tax base to spatially-coded tax policy parameters. The section will conclude with a discussion of the recent empirical research on the impact of local tax differentials and fiscal incentives on the location of business.

3.1 Causal Estimation Of Spatial Tax Reaction Functions

It has been common in the past couple of decades to address the issue of whether decentralized authorities interact strategically with each other in fiscal policy making by estimating a spatial tax reaction function. The spatial tax reaction function allows the observations of a tax policy at a number of relevant spatial locations (states, regions, or municipalities) to be determined simultaneously as the vector of tax policy realizations in contiguous or related localities through a first- or higher-order spatial auto-regressive model that is assumed to accurately describe the underlying data generating process.

In fact, ascertaining whether the geographical location of local authorities plays a role in tax setting –say, due to imperfect mobility of the tax base or to local information spillovers – has proved to be an extremely challenging exercise for a number of reasons. First, in the presence of geographically coded observations on variables that describe interesting economic phenomena or public finance instruments and that might be hard to assume independent of one another, characterizing and interpreting the dependence among those observations necessarily requires imposing restrictions on the process linking the observations at various locations. Given that estimating the full variance-covariance structure is not feasible, the conventional spatial econometrics approach consists in imposing a priori a spatial weights matrix postulating the links – or the absence of links – between any two pairs of observations, along with estimating the extent of spatial auto-correlation among units conditional on that specific spatial structure (Gibbons and Overman, 2012). Second, estimating the effect that the realization of a given variable has on the realizations of that variable in related locations requires addressing properly the inherent simultaneity issue. Finally, one can think of a number of ways that events occurring at nearby locations might not be independent. These include an endogenous interaction effect, by which the behavior of a policy maker at a given location affects the behavior of other policy makers in related locations, or an exogenous effect arising from the impact of the average underlying traits of the "neighborhood" on individual outcomes, or to "correlated effects" due to unobserved characteristics driving agents' behavior (Manski, 1993). Identification of the parameters capturing those effects will tend to be difficult in most circumstances.

In order to allow identification and causal interpretation of the estimated spatial interaction parameters, and to overcome the physiological lack of valid instruments for neighboring jurisdictions' policies (Gibbons and Overman, 2012), some recent research into the estimation of spatial fiscal reaction functions has focused on the search for sources of exogenous variation in spatially linked locations. In fact, relying on the characteristics of neighboring localities as instruments for neighbors' policies has proved to deliver weak or invalid instruments in some circumstances.[5] To see why it is so important to carefully design the approach for estimation of the reaction function, consider the spatial Durbin specification that has been increasingly used in applied spatial econometrics work (Breuillé and Le Gallo, 2017; Delgado et al., 2018). The increased popularity of that specification (equation (6)) is based on the argument that it nests two commonly used empirical models, the conventional spatial lag model and the spatial error model:

$$\mathbf{Y} = \rho \mathbf{W} \mathbf{Y} + \mathbf{X} \boldsymbol{\beta} + \mathbf{W} \mathbf{X} \boldsymbol{\theta} + \boldsymbol{\varepsilon} \tag{6}$$

where, in a cross-sectional context, $\mathbf{Y}$ is a $(N \times 1)$ vector containing observations on the variable of interest, $\mathbf{X}$ is a $(N \times K)$ matrix of exogenous determinants of $\mathbf{Y}$, and $\mathbf{W}$ is a $(N \times N)$ matrix containing information on the spatial location of observations. Element w_{ij} of matrix $\mathbf{W}$ is different from zero if locations i and j are neighbors according to the prespecified "neighborhood"

---

[5] An alternative way of tackling the simultaneity of own and neighboring authorities' fiscal decisions is to measure the latter with a time lag in the spatial reaction function (Buettner and von Schwerin, 2016; Chirinko and Wilson, 2017).

criterion. ρ (with $0 < |\rho| < 1$) is the crucial spatial auto-correlation coefficient that can be interpreted as the "slope" of the fiscal reaction function, and $\beta' = [\beta_1, \ldots, \beta_K]'$ and $\theta' = [\theta_1, \ldots, \theta_K]'$ are $(1 \times K)$ vectors of coefficients to be estimated. Importantly, the N^2 elements of $\mathbf{W}$ cannot be estimated because of lack of degrees of freedom, so that they have to be set a priori based on theoretical considerations or previous evidence. Setting $\theta = 0$ in (6) delivers the spatial lag specification, where the only way neighbors' observed characteristics can affect own policies is through neighbors' polices – that is, the model which has traditionally been seen as the straightforward empirical analog of the tax reaction function from theoretical models of tax competition for mobile capital (Cassette et al., 2012; Freret and Maguain, 2017; Wang, 2018):

$$\mathbf{Y} = \rho\mathbf{W}\mathbf{Y} + \mathbf{X}\boldsymbol{\beta} + \boldsymbol{\varepsilon} \tag{7}$$

In particular, the effect of a change in an exogenous variable $k = 1, \ldots, K$ at any given location $j(\Delta x_{kj})$ has an impact on the whole vector of the dependent variable $\mathbf{Y} = \{y_i\}$ that is given by $\partial y_i/\partial x_{kj} = \mathbf{M}_\rho(i,j)\beta_k, i = 1, \ldots, N$, where $\mathbf{M}_\rho(i,j)$ is the $(i,j)^{th}$ off-diagonal element of matrix $\mathbf{M}_\rho$:

$$E(\mathbf{Y}|\mathbf{X}) = (\mathbf{I}-\rho\mathbf{W})^{-1}\mathbf{X}\beta = M_\rho\mathbf{X}\boldsymbol{\beta} \tag{8}$$

On the other hand, imposing $\theta = -\rho\boldsymbol{\beta}$ generates a linear regression model with a spatial autoregressive process in the residuals, the spatial error model:

$$\mathbf{Y} = \mathbf{X}\boldsymbol{\beta} + \boldsymbol{\varepsilon} \tag{9}$$

$$\boldsymbol{\varepsilon} = \rho\mathbf{W}\boldsymbol{\varepsilon} + \mathbf{u} \tag{10}$$

where $\mathbf{u}$ is independently and identically distributed, and OLS estimation of (9) ignoring the spatial process in (10) yields consistent though inefficient estimates of the parameter vector $\boldsymbol{\beta}$. Consistent two-stage-least-squares estimation of equation (7) requires instead that neighbors' characteristics $\mathbf{W}\mathbf{X}$ be correctly excluded from the second stage equation, and be used as instruments for $\mathbf{W}\mathbf{Y}$ in the first stage.

Similarly, even though all parameters in the most general specification of the spatial reaction function in equation (6) are in theory identified, consistent estimation of the parameter vector $(\rho, \boldsymbol{\beta}, \boldsymbol{\theta})$ requires that the spatial weights matrix $\mathbf{W}$ be correctly specified for higher-order spatial lags of $\mathbf{X}(\mathbf{W}^2\mathbf{X}, \mathbf{W}^3\mathbf{X}, \ldots)$ to satisfy the exclusion restrictions and be valid instruments for $\mathbf{W}\mathbf{Y}$. However, it is unclear how to evaluate the hypotheses on the spatial structure of the process (the composition of matrix $\mathbf{W}$) that are needed to generate the set of instruments, a problem that becomes even more serious if one allows ε itself to have a spatial structure in equations (6) and (7), or if any of the assumed exogenous variables in $\mathbf{X}$ are not so.

As a result, credible identification of the causal impact of the spatial lag of the endogenous variable **WY** *on* **Y** is increasingly obtained by exploiting exogenous shocks to neighbors' policies. These can arise from changes in rules, limits, and resource distribution mechanisms having an impact on **WY**, while having no direct effect on **Y**. Lyytikainen (2012) represents one of the first attempts in this direction. He makes use of a local public finance reform that occurred in Finland in 2000 and raised the upper and lower limits that the central government imposed on local governments' property tax rates. For all authorities that in 1999 were setting a lower tax rate than the new limit, the reform generated exogenous and large tax rate changes, given that the new limit was almost twice as large as the previous one and affected about a third of the authorities. Those forced increases can be taken as the required source of exogenous variation and can be used as instruments for changes in neighbors' tax rates in a spatial lag specification of a property tax rate determination equation. In the empirical implementation of his approach, Lyytikainen (2012) realizes that corner solutions arise when authorities are against the new lower limit in the year 2000, thus complicating the estimation of the spatial reaction function (Di Porto and Revelli, 2013). Consequently, he focuses on the behavior of municipalities for which the new lower limit is not binding by dropping the corner solution observations, and estimates the response of those unconstrained authorities to the tax rate changes in *all* neighboring authorities, regardless of whether they are constrained by the new limit using the predicted imposed tax rate increases corresponding to corner solution observations as instruments. The empirical analysis conducted on the differenced cross-section 1999–2000 reveals virtually no response of unconstrained authorities to tax rate changes taking place in the neighborhood.

Following a similar logic, Isen (2014) exploits the widespread use of referenda by local governments imposed by state law in Ohio for the determination of taxation and public spending to overcome the problem of simultaneous determination of own and neighboring authorities' fiscal decisions in the fiscal reaction function. In particular, Isen (2014) adopts a regression discontinuity approach, in the sense that he exploits the outcomes of "close" referenda, where one can assume a quasi-random assignment of "treatment" to fiscal decisions of neighbors that just passed the approval threshold relative to the measures that just narrowly failed to pass. Using purely geographic as well as migration-based and socio-demographic similarity criteria of proximity between local jurisdictions (counties, municipalities, school districts) and employing a number of distinct dependent variables (rates, revenues, expenditures), Isen (2014) finds no evidence of fiscal interaction. Interestingly, when the same data are used to estimate a fiscal reaction function by means of an instrumental variables approach using neighbors' socio-demographic characteristics as instruments for neighbors' fiscal policies, the estimates of the spatial interaction effects turn out to be large and statistically significant.

Baskaran (2014) adopts a similar approach in order to estimate a reaction function for local government fiscal policies. He analyzes the impact of reform in a German state, using a nearby state as control. In particular, he exploits the exogenous reform of the local fiscal equalization scheme in the German state of North Rhine-Westphalia to study the mimicking behavior by the authorities in the neighboring state of Lower Saxony, which was not directly affected by the reform. The exogenous shock to the former authorities, which were induced to raise their tax rates by the reform, is used to identify the presence of fiscal interactions by overcoming the issues of simultaneous determination and endogeneity that typically arise in studies of this type. Baskaran (2014) finds no evidence of tax mimicking when using the exogenous variation caused by the reform as instruments, irrespective of the weighting scheme used. On the other hand, he also finds that the estimation of a tax reaction function that uses neighboring authorities' demographic and political characteristics as instruments for their tax policies returns evidence of strategic interaction that might in reality be caused by the use of invalid instruments.

Finally, Parchet (2019) tackles the issue of the sign of an income tax reaction function in a multi-tiered structure of government. First, his theoretical model shows that the slope of the local tax reaction function can either be positive (tax rates of competing jurisdictions are strategic complements) or negative (strategic substitutes), and highlights the factors that determine the sign in terms of economies of scale in the production of the public good and the elasticity of the marginal utility of the public good. He then exploits the discontinuity at internal cantonal Swiss borders to estimate a local income tax reaction function, where neighboring localities' income tax rates across the border are instrumented with the upper level of government (cantonal) tax rate. The idea is that tax policies at the cantonal level provide a one-way and arguably exogenous source of variation for the tax rate set by the local level of government, and that taxpayers close to the cantonal border are potentially mobile and make their decisions in response to the total tax rate (municipal + cantonal) on their incomes. He estimates a linear spatial reaction function where the consolidated local-plus-cantonal income tax rate measured at the municipal level is allowed to depend on the weighted average of the consolidated local-plus-cantonal income tax rates of neighboring municipalities that are possibly located in different cantons. Using neighboring cantonal tax rates multiplied by the share of municipalities located in those cantons as instruments for average consolidated neighbors' tax rates, the key interaction coefficient turns out to be negative, pointing to income tax rates being strategic substitutes. While the idea of using upper-tier tax rates as instruments for consolidated neighbors' tax rates in the vicinity of borders is interesting, doing so requires imposing a set of restrictions on the original reaction function (such as the equality of the response of a municipality's tax rate to nearby municipalities', own canton's, and neighboring cantons' tax policies) that seem unlikely to be satisfied in most circumstances.

3.2 Tax Base Responses to Local Fiscal Policy Differentials

In general, evidence of horizontal fiscal interaction between neighboring tax-setting authorities can arise from a number of alternative political-economic mechanisms. These include competition for mobile tax bases, interjurisdictional flows of information in the presence of comparative performance evaluation of governments on the part of voters inducing policy makers to mimic each other's policies (yardstick competition), or spillovers from the provision of public services and infrastructures benefitting residents in nearby localities (Brueckner, 2003). Indeed, the mobility of households in a decentralized public sector structure has attracted an enormous interest due to its potential of leading to an efficient provision of local public goods and an optimal allocation of households to communities (Tiebout, 1956). On the other hand, the differential net fiscal benefits for citizens, depending on the fiscal capacities of their place of residence that arise in fiscally decentralized structures, tend to lead both to horizontal inequity and to inefficient migration (Boadway and Flatters, 1982). From an empirical point of view, though, addressing the issue of whether decentralized fiscal policies play a significant role in households' internal migration decisions besides the well-established "push and pull" factors from labor market conditions and environmental amenities has proved problematic, thwarted by endogeneity, reverse causality, and measurement issues (Kuminoff et al., 2013).

Early ways of overcoming the policy endogeneity problem have been to use household-level data and employ microeconometric techniques to identify the variables affecting individual decisions of where to reside (Schmidheiny, 2006; Liebig and Sousa-Poza, 2006; Liebig, Puhani, and Sousa-Poza, 2007). More recently, an increasing number of papers rely on quasi-experimental circumstances where local tax policies change exogenously in the proximity of internal borders in order to identify the effect of decentralized fiscal policy on households' location decisions.

3.2.1 Income Tax Policy and Taxpayers' Mobility: Border Discontinuities and Quasi-Experimental Studies

In the absence of formal or substantive barriers to internal migration, the taxation of personal income in principle can exert a decisive influence on the location of households – particularly those at the upper end of the income distribution.[6] The major econometric issue that researchers need to tackle when studying the impact of local income taxation on the location of households is that of reverse causality: the tax income schedule that a locality can afford to set depends itself on the income distribution of the population that resides in that jurisdiction. A growing recent literature attempts at identifying the impact of the local tax structure on individual location decisions by exploiting exogenous shocks to local income taxation schedules.[7] These shocks can arise either from the presence of higher-level administrative units that create discontinuities at internal borders, or from the existence of legal thresholds in the computation of income tax liabilities, or from spatially limited reforms creating geographically defined control and treatment groups. These studies generally uncover large and precisely estimated elasticities of internal migration flows to local income tax policy differentials.

Martinez (2017) analyzes the impact of a regressive income tax reform in the canton of Obwalden (central Switzerland) in 2006 on taxpayers' location decisions, using individual income tax data and exact moving dates. The reform, approved by popular referendum, changed the existing flat income tax schedule into a regressive tax scheme (declining marginal income tax rates for a range of high incomes) that mostly benefitted taxpayers in the top 1% of the income distribution in the first two years. A federal court rule later imposed the return to a flat income tax rate, though the canton chose a lower level than the preexisting one, in 2008. Martinez (2017) shows by a difference-in-differences approach using nearby cantons as controls that the share of high-income taxpayers in the canton and the level of taxable income per taxpayer both raised after the reform. When investigating the mechanism leading to those results, she finds that the effect is mostly due to rich taxpayers moving in – a phenomenon facilitated by

---

[6] Here we will not cover the issue of tax-induced international mobility of top earners and the instances of preferential tax treatment to incoming foreigners that may lead to income tax competition and "race to the bottom" policies at the international level (Kleven et al., 2014).

[7] Indeed, other taxes might play a role too. Brulhart and Parchet (2014) study bequest taxation by the Swiss cantonal governmental units, observing that those traditionally high and diverse bequest taxes have been narrowing and falling over time starting from the 1980s. Using a long panel data set through four decades (1970s to 200s), they estimate the elasticity of a number of indicators of tax base (number, income, and tax revenues from retired taxpayers) to own cantonal bequest tax rates and to the average bequest tax rate in neighboring cantons. Their empirical analysis provides no compelling evidence that the tax base elasticity to bequest tax policy was responsible for the race to the bottom that occurred in Switzerland over time.

the lack of cultural barriers, the small distances between cantons, and the absence of legal restrictions. From the point of view of cantonal revenues, though, the reform was roughly revenue neutral.

Basten, Ehrlich, and Lassmann (2017) estimate the elasticity of housing rents to local income tax differentials by means of a discrete choice model where households sort into localities according to their incomes, tastes for housing, taxes, and neighborhood characteristics. Based on detailed information on all residences advertised for rent in Switzerland over the years 2005–2012, as well as on individual socio-demographics characteristics and taxable income data, they adopt a boundary discontinuity design. This implies comparing close-by residences sharing the same amenities and neighborhood characteristics, but facing different local income taxes because of being located on either side of an inter-municipal border. First, they find that the rent elasticity to the local income tax rate is about –0.3, corresponding to two-thirds of house price capitalization estimates from conventional hedonic regression models that might not fully account for unobserved location and neighborhood characteristics.[8] Second, their evidence points to household spatial sorting according to income. High-income households are willing to pay higher rents than poorer ones for residing in neighborhoods that are wealthier, that have lower income taxes, and that require lower moving distance, consistent with the hypothesis of non-homothetic preferences.

Schmidheiny and Slotwinski (2018) study the tax-induced behavior of high-income foreigners in Switzerland. They exploit a special regulation in the Swiss tax law according to which foreigners with gross income below a threshold pay a fixed cantonal rate for the first five years of stay, while those above the threshold are immediately subject to the ordinary regime, that has variation in tax rates (local multipliers applied on cantonal rates) across municipalities. The existence of the income threshold and of the duration threshold makes it possible to employ regression discontinuity designs. First, they hypothesize that newly arrived foreigners with income below the threshold should choose to locate in high tax municipalities, because they can enjoy the lower housing prices while not being subject to the high-income tax rates because of the special fiscal regime. On the other hand, foreigners with income above the threshold should choose to locate in low tax municipalities to minimize their tax burden. In addition, one should observe taxpayers adjusting their income around those "notches." In fact, foreigners in high tax municipalities tend to lower their income just below the threshold to enjoy the special fiscal regime. Those in

---

[8] Hilber (2011) provides an excellent review of the voluminous literature on capitalization of taxes and public services in property prices and housing rents.

low tax municipalities lift their income just above the threshold to get into the ordinary taxation scheme. Given that the special regime expires after five years, the expectation is that high-income foreigners in high-tax municipalities will choose to relocate to low-tax municipalities when the special regime expires, while those located in low-tax municipalities are likely to stay. Using detailed data on location decisions, income, labor market conditions, and socio-demographics from individuals that are eligible for the special tax scheme, they find evidence that local tax differences can induce internal mobility of foreigners that would otherwise experience a tax rise, with the probability of moving being increasing in the expected returns from relocation.

Agrawal and Foremny (2019) study a fiscal decentralization reform in Spain that allowed regions to set their own residence-based personal income tax rates and brackets, and estimate its effect on the mobility of individual taxpayers during the period 2005–2014. The reform led to large marginal tax rate differentials, particularly on high-income taxpayers, and raised worries that tax-induced mobility of wealthy taxpayers would make redistribution unfeasible. Based on sample data of taxpayers from Social Security records, and using individual movers' data, they find a significant impact of regional taxes on location choices. A 1% increase in the net of tax rate in a region raises the probability of moving to that region by 1.7 percentage points. In an aggregate region-by-region pairwise analysis that allows estimation of the stock elasticity of the population of top-income taxpayers in a region with respect to its own net-of-average-tax-rate, the elasticity is estimated to be around 0.85. In order to simulate the revenue impact of an income tax policy change that raises the marginal income tax rate on incomes above the highest income bracket while leaving all other rates unchanged, they decompose the total effect into three effects. The first is a mechanical revenue increase from raising the tax rate, the second is a behavioral one coming from changes in taxable income that depends on the taxable income elasticity, and the third is the mobility effect depending on the stock elasticity of migration. They show that the (positive) mechanical effect from raising the top marginal tax rate largely dominates the other two (negative) effects in all Spanish regions, thus making the prospect of a race-to-the-bottom in top income taxation and of unsustainability of local systems of income redistribution implausible.

Eugster and Parchet (2019) analyze theoretically and empirically the constraints created by tax base mobility between proximate jurisdictions that prevent decentralized governments from selecting their "culturally desired" fiscal policies. Even if nearby jurisdictions have persistent and measurable differences in preferences over publicly provided goods that should lead to significantly different tax policies, the fact of being spatially close might reduce their tax differentials through competition for mobile and heterogeneous individuals.[9] Empirically, they employ a difference-in-differences approach to identify the existence of tax competition that is based on the comparison of tax differentials between jurisdictions that share a border at which preferences change discontinuously (e.g., French-speaking and German-speaking municipalities in bilingual cantons in Switzerland), with jurisdictions that illustrate analogous differences in preferences but are located far apart on opposite sides of the language border. Exploiting the fact that direct democracy institutions are used frequently in Switzerland and allow to elicit people's preferences on a number of crucial issues, they proxy preferences by the share of support for leftist/progressive referenda. Their results suggest that competition tends to offset culture-related tax differentials: at the language border, the difference-in-difference estimate of the impact of vicinity to the language border on the tax differential is large and highly significant, making the observed tax policies on either side of the border remarkably similar, while the corresponding estimate for the preference proxy differential is zero. Moreover, the difference-in-difference estimate of the border on the tax differential is virtually unaffected when controlling for the preference (vote share) proxies. This suggests that the smooth tax gradient that is observed around the language border cannot be explained by mere people's sorting, but is rather the outcome of strategic behavior of local governments anticipating the sorting of heterogeneous individuals.

As far as the United States is concerned, Young and Warner (2011) and Young et al. (2016) study the outmigration impact of the imposition of state-level "millionaire taxes" on top income earners. Their results generally suggest little responsiveness of the tax base, with estimated elasticities that are small and only marginally significant either when analyzing a specific New Jersey tax that raised the tax rate on top incomes by 2.6 percentage points, or when looking at all million-dollar income earners in the United States for more than a decade. On the other hand, Moretti and Wilson (2017) use data on US state personal income tax, corporate income tax, R&D tax credits, and investment tax credits to estimate to what extent the geographical allocation of highly skilled workers (star scientists) is affected by the large time-series and cross-sectional variation in fiscal burdens. In particular, to control for long-standing state characteristics

---

[9] Parchet (2019) estimates the elasticity of the income tax base to local income tax rate differentials in order to evaluate whether the evidence of Swiss municipalities' income tax rates being strategic substitutes is compatible with a theoretical model of competition for mobile taxpayers' income. Using a panel data set of pairwise cross-canton spatial differences between municipalities at the cantonal border, and instrumenting the spatial difference of the consolidated tax rates with the lagged tax differential of the cantons' tax rates, he gets an income tax base elasticity of about 0.4.

that can produce a spurious correlation between tax rates and the number of highly skilled workers, they estimate the elasticity of migration to fiscal-related incentives by regressing changes in the number of scientists moving between states on the interstate tax differentials. They find significant and large elasticities of the flow of scientists with respect to personal as well as corporate taxes and investment tax credits.

Finally, Milligan and Smart (2019) develop a model of cross-border income shifting in response to subnational income tax differentials in a federation. They show that the optimal tax rates depend on the elasticity of national tax avoidance and of tax base shifting between the units of the federation, and test the model's predictions on data on top income shares and tax rates from the Canadian provinces. In order to address the issue of provincial tax rates' endogeneity, Milligan and Smart (2019) exploit a federal reform that occurred in year 2000 that decentralized income taxation power to the provinces. They combine the postreform dummy with a time-invariant index of province-level concentration of revenues from natural resources (average share of resource revenues over total revenues in the sample period 1988–2013). The idea is that the reform would allow provincial authorities to cut marginal tax rates and the degree of income tax progressivity, depending on the availability of other "exogenous' revenues. Their estimates suggest that the provincial income tax base is highly sensitive to individual provinces' tax changes due to the possibility of income shifting, while the avoidance elasticity is relatively small, implying little tax base shrink in response to a nationwide income tax change.

3.2.2 Business Responses to Local Tax Differentials

Besides the impact of local income taxation on the location of households, to what extent decentralized business tax policies influence the location of productive establishments, investment, and employment has been a traditional research question within the empirical fiscal federalism literature. The early evidence based on longitudinal observations at large spatial units (US states) typically failed to unveil a large impact of taxes on states' economic performance, fueling skepticism about the ability of tax breaks and investment tax credits alone to stimulate state economic development (Bartik, 1985). However, it is by now well known that empirical research into the impact of tax policy on economic activity is plagued by endogeneity problems, making it prohibitive to estimate the effect of taxes on the economy correctly. Given that fiscal policy is determined by current or prospective economic conditions, macro approaches relying on administrative data require exogenous sources of policy variation in order to identify the causal effect of public policy on the economy (Barro and Redlick, 2011).

The policy endogeneity problem has been tackled in a number of ways. First, based on the early approach proposed by Holmes (1998) and mirroring the work on decentralized personal income taxation, a number of authors have recurred to spatial discontinuities at borders using smaller spatial aggregates such as the US counties (Chirinko and Wilson, 2008). Moreover, thanks to the increasing availability of large micro data sets on the location and characteristics of firms, a number of authors have employed geocoded information on productive establishments to investigate the impact of local taxes and fiscal incentives on micro-level business location decisions (Devereux, Griffith, and Simpson, 2007; Rathelot and Sillard, 2008).[10] As argued by Duranton, Gobillon, and Overman (2011), though, three main issues need to be addressed when employing micro-data on firms or plants to infer the economic impact of local tax differentials. The first is the likely presence of unobserved location-specific effects that might be correlated with important explanatory variables, such as plant characteristics, or with the very local fiscal variables that are the crucial object of interest of the analysis. Second, there are establishment-specific effects that might lead firms to sort to specific locations because of those characteristics, thus likely producing a selection bias. Finally, there might be an endogeneity of local tax setting decisions leading to a reverse causality bias. Duranton, Gobillon, and Overman (2011) propose an econometric approach that is based on spatial differencing (to deal with unobserved location-specific effects), time differencing (to deal with establishment-specific effects), and a set of instrumental variables (changes in party control of the local council) to tackle the local tax policy endogeneity issue. Using data on English manufacturing establishments and local politics, they find a negative impact of local taxation on employment but no effect on the location of new plants.

Belotti, Di Porto, and Santoni (2016) apply the pairwise spatial differenced instrumental variable methodology built by Duranton, Gobillon, and Overman (2011) to a panel data set of Italian manufacturing firms that contains their geographical coordinates to investigate the impact of municipal nonresidential property taxation on a number of indicators of business performance. Using political alignment between municipal governments and central government as

---

[10] Brulhart, Jametti, and Schmidheiny (2012) study the effects of corporate taxes on firm births using panel data on new firm counts per municipality and economic sector in Switzerland, focusing on the impact of agglomeration economies on the sensitivity of firms to local tax differentials. The role of agglomeration economies has attracted a considerable interest in the urban economics literature, as shown in the recent review chapter by Brulhart, Bucovetsky, and Schmidheiny (2015).

instrument for municipal fiscal choices, they find a negative and significant impact of local taxes on sales, capital, employment, and total factor productivity.

In order to estimate the impact of a US investment tax credit, the New Markets Tax Credit (NMTC), Harger and Ross (2016) exploit the fact that eligibility of a local area to the NMTC is based on the ratio of the census tract median family income to the state median income not exceeding 0.80. They compare business activity in census tracts that just qualified to those that just failed, thus controlling for common unobserved local attributes. They find that most of the effect was an expansion of existing plants rather than the entry of new firms.

An alternative approach to deal with fiscal policy endogeneity is to exploit the circumstances where a tax increase can be considered exogenous because it is motivated by "an inherited budget deficit" (Romer and Romer, 2010) or is "enforced by external bodies" (Cloyne, 2013). Following that argument, Revelli (2015b) makes use of a top-down mandate on financially distressed local authorities in Italy, and investigates the impact on factor input use of the centrally mandated regional business income tax rate increases in the regions with excessive public debt. The empirical strategy relies on the abrupt change in central government policy toward those regions that occurred after the 2005 regional elections, making the tax mandates exogenous with respect to the evolution of regional economic conditions. The estimation results reveal that mandated business tax hikes had a significant detrimental impact on regional employment but provide no evidence of major shifts of production facilities or variable input use from high-tax to low-tax localities.

Finally, Liu and Martinez-Vasquez (2014) adopt a structural form approach to analyze the elasticity of the business tax base in Chinese provinces (measured as the ratio of foreign direct investments to GDP of a province in a panel data set on 30 provinces for the period 1983–2007) to the provincial average effective tax rate. In turn, the average effective tax rate is allowed to depend in an auxiliary spatial equation on the tax rates set by neighboring provinces and on whether there exist development zones in the province. The latter are special government-designated areas that aim at attracting foreign investments and transfer of technology by means of a number of fiscal advantages including a lower corporate income tax rate. Development zones have grown impressively since their introduction in the 1980s, and they are considered in the paper as the main tool by which provinces compete with each other to attract investment. The results from three-stage-least-squares (3SLS) estimation of the dynamic system suggest that the introduction of development zones is accompanied by a significant reduction of the average effective tax rate in a province that in turn attracts more foreign direct investments.

4 Vertical Fiscal Competition

As Keen pointed out more than two decades ago, "the essence of federalism is multi-leveled government," (Keen, 1998: 454) and a key aspect of fiscal arrangements in federations is the "concurrent taxation of the same tax bases by federal and state government" (Keen, 1998: 454). Besides the horizontal fiscal externalities that have been the focus of most of the research in the field of fiscal federalism, the existence of overlapping tiers of government taxing concurrently the same economic activities generates the potential dependence of the tax base of each level of government on the tax policies of the other governments through the private sector's responses. In turn, this dependence can spur vertical tax competition, with tax policies at each level of government reacting to the tax policies set at the other levels. Apart from those fiscal spillovers from the revenue side of the budget, though, there can also be an interaction from the expenditure side of the budget between governments at different tiers that provide public goods that might be complementary or substitutes in taxpayers' utility functions. This implies that there can be numerous channels of vertical interaction, that the sign of the various forms of dependence will be ex ante indeterminate, and that it will be difficult to separately identify them in most circumstances. In addition, it is most likely that vertical fiscal interactions will occur at the same time as horizontal ones, possibly at all existing tiers of government, making the simultaneous analysis of all these forms of externalities and interdependencies particularly challenging (Goodspeed, 2000; Brulhart and Jametti, 2006).

To see how vertical fiscal interactions emerge, consider the following simple representation of a two-tiered structure of government, with each tier being composed of multiple authorities having taxation power on a number of bases and providing a public good, and with each unit at the upper tier containing several units of the lower tier. The fundamental intuitions from the works of Boadway and Keen (1996), Keen (1998), and Besley and Rosen (1998) apply to this "multi-federation" (Agrawal, 2016) and "multi-revenue" (Perez-Sebastian and Raveh, 2018) institutional environment. These recent extensions of the basic one-federation and one-tax to several upper-level units and many revenue instruments make it possible to deal with a more realistic empirical framework and allow for a number of different useful specifications of the vertical fiscal reaction functions.

In particular, let R be the number of units of government at the upper tier, and let them be indexed by $r = 1, \ldots, R$. They can be viewed as states in a federal country or regions in a unitary one. They are large and move first relative to lower-tier authorities. Each of those units is, in turn, subdivided into M small-sized local governments, indexed by $m = 1, \ldots, M$, that can be viewed as districts or municipalities. Each municipality m located in region r sets a vector of H tax rates $t_{mr} = [t_{mr1}, t_{mr2}, \ldots , t_{mrH}]$ on the vector of imperfectly mobile tax bases $b_{mr} = [b_{mr1}, b_{mr2}, \ldots , b_{mrH}]$ that are located within their municipal boundaries. Moreover, each municipality provides a local public good that enters the utility function of residents of the municipality only, with no horizontal spillovers. To keep the set-up as simple as possible, here we ignore the common feature of vertical intergovernmental transfers and assume that municipal expenditures on the public good (g_{mr}) must be financed entirely by own tax revenues according to a balanced budget rule: $\Sigma t_{mrh} b_{mrh} = g_{mr}$. Similarly, each region r sets the vector of H tax rates $T_r = [T_{r1}, T_{r2}, \ldots , T_{rH}]$ on the tax bases $B_r = [B_{r1}, B_{r2}, \ldots , B_{rH}]$, where $\sum b_{mrh} = B_{rh}$ when summing over all municipalities in the region, and uses its tax revenues to provide a region-wide public good: $\sum T_{rh} B_{rh} = G_r$, with no interregional spillovers. The public goods provided by the two overlapping levels of government enter the utility function of the residents of municipality m along with private consumption c_{mr}:

$$W_{mr} = u(c_{mr}) + q(g_{mr}, G_r) \tag{11}$$

where u and q are increasing concave functions. Assume that municipal government m sets the tax rate vector t_{mr} to maximize welfare subject to its budget constraint, and taking the fiscal choices of the upper levels of government as given. The first order conditions for each of the tax rates t_{mrh}, establishing the equality between the marginal cost and the marginal benefit of raising revenues through tax instrument $h = 1, \ldots , H$, are

$$\partial u(c_{mr})/\partial t_{mrh} + \gamma[\partial q(g_{mr}, G_r)/\partial g_{mr}] = 0 \tag{12}$$

where, using the municipal budget constraint and letting ε_{hh} and ε_{kh} be the own and cross tax base elasticities with respect to tax rate t_{mrh},

$$\gamma \equiv \partial g_{mr}/\partial t_{mrh} = t_{mrh}(1 + \varepsilon_{hh}) + \sum\nolimits_{k \neq h}(t_{mrk}/t_{mrh})\varepsilon_{kh} \tag{13}$$

By totally differentiating (12), ignoring any horizontal fiscal externality, and rearranging, one obtains the following "vertical" tax reaction functions:

$$dt_{mrh}/dT_{rk} = -(1/\theta)\{\partial^2 u(c_{mr})/\partial t_{mrh}T_{rk} + [\partial q(g_{mr}, G_r)/\partial g_{mr}](\partial \gamma/\partial T_{rk})$$

$$+\gamma[\partial^2 q(g_{mr}, G_r)/\partial g_{mr}\partial T_{rk}]\} \tag{14}$$

$$dt_{mrh}/dT_{sk} = -(1/\vartheta)\{\partial^2 u(c_{mr})/\partial t_{mrh}\partial T_{sk} + [\partial q(g_{mr}, G_r)/\partial g_{mr}](\partial \gamma/\partial T_{sk})\} \tag{15}$$

where, because of concavity of the objective function,

$$\theta = \partial/\partial t_{mrh}[\partial u(c_{mr})/\partial t_{mrh} + \gamma\left(\partial q(g_{mr}, G_r)/\partial g_{mr}\right)] < 0 \qquad (16)$$

The reaction function (14) concerns the direct impact on the tax rate on base h of municipality m belonging to region r of region r's tax rate setting policy on tax base k, where k can be the same or a different tax base than h. It contains three terms: the first arises because a change in the upper level authority's tax rate determines a change in the local tax rate, and therefore on private consumption of residents in municipality m; the second arises from the fact that the tax base change has an impact on the municipal public good that can be provided by m; and finally, the change in the upper level tax rate brings about a change in the upper level authority's provision of public good G that can be a complement or a substitute of the municipal public good g.

The reaction function (15) allows for an effect from taxation of base k from a nearby regional government $s \neq r$ on taxation of tax base h by a municipality m belonging to region r. Since municipality m does not belong to region s, this effect has been dubbed a "diagonal" externality (Agrawal, 2016). The reaction function contains only two terms, that is the terms referring to the tax base externality, under the assumption that the public good provided by region s has no impact on the welfare of region r's residents. In both cases (14) and (15), the sign of the reaction function is indeterminate, as all effects can go in either direction.

The early empirical literature on vertical tax competition focused on corporate income taxes, personal income taxes, and excise duties (gasoline, cigarettes) in federal countries, and was promptly followed by analyses of multilevel property tax setting and correlation between public expenditures at the regional and local level in unitary countries.[11] The most recent research has made increasing attempts at tackling the endogeneity of fiscal policy changes at overlapping layers of government, and has further improved on early attempts at incorporating vertical fiscal externalities in empirical models of horizontal fiscal competition for mobile resources at "internal" federal borders. It is to these more recent pieces of research that the remainder of this section is devoted.

Agrawal (2014) studies the time and spatial dynamics of local option sales taxes (LOST) using high-frequency (monthly) data on US state and local governments. Besides documenting a number of interesting facts about the evolution of the practical implementation of LOST, Agrawal (2014) builds state-level indexes of local sales taxation that allow him to study competition

---

[11] See the extensive reviews in Revelli (2006) and Revelli (2015a).

among states in selecting "tax systems." This means that the indicators of state tax burdens fully include the taxation efforts of sub-state governments that are constrained by the rules set by state governments themselves. The argument is that any investigation of cross-border shopping, business location decision and tax incidence cannot overlook the important role of local sales tax rates in addition to state rates, and the power that states have in determining the degree of importance and flexibility of the LOST system. He then estimates a spatial econometric model based on a spatial Durbin specification that has as dependent variable either the state tax rate, the total tax rate (state plus average local), or the local tax rate as well as its specific components (county, town, district). The evidence, in particular the fact that the "local tax system" as a whole shows stronger spatial association than its individual components, is compatible with the hypothesis that states compete with each other not only by setting their own rates, but by determining the overall state tax system by means of the constraints, they are able to impose onto the local governments that are located within their boundaries.

In subsequent work, Agrawal (2016) analyzes theoretically and empirically the setting of local sales taxes that influence the location of retail activity in a multiple-federations setup – that is, an environment with multiple higher-level local governments (counties) competing with each other, each being in turn composed of many lower-level governments (cities and towns). This leads to the emergence of a number of interfederation horizontal interactions (counties competing with other counties; lower-level authorities in a federation competing with lower-level authorities in other federations), intrafederation competition (vertical fiscal externalities between lower-level and upper-level authority within a federation because of sharing of the same tax base; competition between towns and districts within the same federation), and "diagonal" interfederation competition. As explained previously, this arises when the tax rates of cities in a federation are set competitively with the county of another federation. An important component of the theoretical model as well as of the empirical analysis is the consideration of the location of a lower-level authority relative to the borders of the federation (central or peripheral). In the implementation of the spatial model, historically determined geographic variables (area and perimeter) are used as instruments for other authorities' policies. The results first show that town tax rates are positively correlated with the tax rates of other towns (horizontal interaction at the lower level), while town and county tax rates are negatively correlated (vertical interaction). As for the diagonal interaction, towns' and neighboring counties' tax rates are positively correlated. In addition, the results show considerable heterogeneity in the shape of the fiscal reaction functions both within and across counties when distance to the county border is explicitly considered: in particular, the negative vertical interaction is stronger for towns near the border, because they are the ones that are most affected by cross-border shopping.[12]

On the other hand, Agrawal (2015) tackles the issue of identification of tax competition effects due to cross-border shopping by moving away from the estimation of conventional tax reaction functions and exploiting instead the notch created by the discontinuity of state tax rates at borders and its expected consequences of lower level governments' fiscal behavior. This allows the use of a quasi-experimental design that overcomes the difficulties that we have outlined above and that are caused by the simultaneity of neighboring governments' tax setting decisions. Agrawal (2015) focuses in particular on the "tax gradient effect" – that is, the impact that the discontinuity at a state border between a low sales tax state and a high sales tax state has on the sales tax policy setting by local governments, depending on their distance (driving time) from the border itself. His theoretical model has two major novel empirical predictions concerning the impact of the border discontinuity. The first is a "level effect": municipal tax rates near the border in a low state tax rate are higher than the corresponding rates on the other, high-tax rate side of the border, thus compensating – almost fully, as turns out in the empirical work – the state tax rate differential. The second is a "gradient effect": moving away from the border in a low tax rate state, municipal sales tax rates should fall (a negative tax gradient); and moving away from the border in a high tax rate state, municipal sales tax rates should rise (a positive tax gradient). The empirical evidence suggests that those effects are significant and economically relevant, and that tax competition arising from cross-border shopping tends to be limited to towns that are within a short travelling distance from the state border. The general lesson from this research is an important one in empirical fiscal federalism research: tax burden differentials between neighboring locations are meaningful in a multi-tiered government structure only if the tax efforts of all relevant government tiers are properly taken into account.

---

[12] Rohlin and Thompson (2018) use a panel data set of cross-border US counties to estimate the employment impact of state and local sales taxes due to cross-border shopping. Using the share of residents working in another state to allow for differential responses to local state tax policy, they find that areas with high levels of cross-border commuting experience the highest impact on employment and payroll from changes in sales tax rates. An increase of 1% in the combined state-county sales tax rate leads to an average fall in employment of about 1% relative to cross-border counties, with the effect being twice as large in counties with high interstate commuting rates and being nil in counties with low interstate commuting rates. In related work, Greenhalgh-Stanley, Rohlin, and Thompson (2018) use a similar approach and data (fixed effects panel data estimates on cross-border US county pairs) to find that food sales taxes have adverse employment effects in the food and beverage stores industry.

Reingewertz (2018) focuses on the vertical tax externality that arises in a federal system when the federal government raises revenues from a tax base that is shared with the states composing the federation. In particular, he studies the effect of federal corporate tax policy on state corporate as well as noncorporate tax revenues, using the narrative-based methodological approach of Romer and Romer (2010) to tackle the potential endogeneity of federal tax policy changes. In particular, following the classification of exogenous tax shocks made by Romer and Romer (2010), he estimates on annual state-level panel data the impact of the federal tax change on the first difference of log state tax revenues in an equation that includes a spatial component represented by the log of the weighted average of neighboring states' tax revenues. In general, the results point to a negative effect of federal tax shocks on state corporate tax revenues, though the magnitude of the effect is relatively small, with the most likely transmission channel being a shrinking tax base due to reduced business activity.

Perez-Sebastian and Raveh (2018) tackle the issue of separately identifying the vertical fiscal externalities arising from the common pool problem due to tax base sharing and those arising from the public expenditure side, in particular from the complementarity or substitutability of public goods provided by different tiers of government. If, say, federal and state public goods are complements – for instance, the federal government invests in interstate highways and state governments provide for side connection roads – then vertical fiscal interactions on the revenue and expenditure sides of the budgets might go in the same direction. This would happen if the higher tax rates set at the federal level to fund those infrastructures prompt higher state tax rates to counterbalance the shrinking tax bases, making it difficult to discriminate between the two channels of transmission from federal to state decision-making empirically. If federal and state public goods are substitutes, then a federal shock in terms of an expenditure boost should induce lower state spending, thus going in the opposite direction as a tax base eroding effect. Perez-Sebastian and Raveh (2018) develop a model where the two channels coexist and establish under what conditions they work in the same or opposite direction. Empirically, they exploit the fact that an increase in a federal tax on a good (oil) that is immobile and only available in some of the states – the 1980 US Crude Oil Windfall Act – creates a tax erosion problem in those oil-rich states only. These circumstances allow them to identify the pure public good complementarity or substitutability effect in the other states by means of a difference-in-differences approach in a quasi-experimental setting, where oil-endowed states constitute the treatment group and the remaining (18) states the control group. The evidence from estimation of a tax reaction function suggests that resource-poor states change their own tax rates (sales and income) in the same direction as the federal tax shock, pointing at complementarity between state and federal public goods. The complementarity effect channel is estimated to account for about 40% of the total effect. As far as tax externalities from tax base erosion are concerned, the evidence suggests a negatively sloped reaction function of state to federal tax policy.

Indeed, with fiscal policy responsibilities being increasingly vertically fragmented in governance structures of growing complexity, the analysis of fiscal interactions between governments at different tiers seems to deserve careful attention in future empirical research. This seems particularly important with reference to large metropolitan areas that see the concentration of economic activity, human capital and innovation, as well as the emergence of issues of congestion, pollution, and social and environmental sustainability, and where regulatory powers, management of key infrastructures for development, and assignments of revenue sources between different levels of government frequently and necessarily overlap.

5 Accountability and Fiscal Policy

In the remaining sections of this Element, we focus on political accountability and credibility in multi-tier settings. Broadly speaking, one may observe how the link between decentralization and accountability has been depicted in two distinct ways in the literature: First, many works address the question of whether decentralization per se helps or hinders accountability. The theoretical predictions in this sense are not conclusive. The original contribution by Oates (1972) sees decentralization as a means to make policies closer to voters' preferences; as long as preference heterogeneity is lower at the local than at the national level and economies of scale are not too strong, then local public good provision ensures higher overall welfare. Weingast (1995) and Seabright (1996) note that the closer link between voters and local politicians may give voters more scope for exit and voice in decentralized places; monitoring may be more effective and less costly at the local level, as local voters may be more empowered and interested in participating in local politics, making decentralized decisions of better *quality* than centralized ones. Second, other authors instead point out that decentralization may be detrimental to accountability. Decentralized systems may be more complicated to navigate for voters: different tiers may have overlapping responsibilities and vertical fiscal gaps, and equalization grants may create a cleavage between local taxation and local spending, lowering the responsibility of politicians for their actions. Prud'homme (1995) notes that institutional monitoring, such as the control by the judiciary or other analogous agencies, may be more effective when it comes to national politics and national politicians, and that local politicians typically have greater discretionary powers, making them more prone to corruption. Local political elites may also be easier (and cheaper) to capture for interest groups (Shleifer and Vishny, 1993; Bardhan and Mookherjee, 2000). More generally, local politicians may hold a stronger monopoly power over voters than national politicians (Kunicová and Rose-Ackerman, 2005).

The main challenge faced by researchers in this area is linked to the difficulty in defining robust identification strategies and the paucity of reliable data sources. The degree of decentralization tends to be quite stable across time in each country and is rooted in the country's history and characteristics. Empirical studies rely on country-level cross-sections (more rarely panels), in which researchers strive to establish a causal link between the degree of decentralization and various measures of government outcomes that may possibly proxy accountability. The research design remains challenging: decentralization and accountability are bound to be correlated with other variables, and establishing a unidirectional causal link is difficult. The fairly stable nature of the institutional arrangements such as decentralization, once again, makes it quite hard to find a credible instrument for decentralization.

From the measurement point of view, both decentralization and government accountability pose challenges. Researchers used proxies for decentralization, such as ad hoc indices based on constitutional protection of local autonomy and revenue or expenditure decentralization; similarly, accountability and government output quality are measured through proxies that are often questionable in their construction. For example, corruption is widely used in cross-country studies as a sign of lack of transparency and accountability in the system. At the same time, reliable measures of corruption are limited; more precisely, most of them are measures of the *perception* of corruption, constructed through surveys of both local stakeholders and "experts" of local conditions.

The other strands of the literature we are going to analyze uses data sets of decentralized (or federated) governments to explore the issue of government accountability and credibility. As already pointed out in the Introduction, the existence of decentralized governments is helpful for researchers for the sheer possibility of doing large-sample analyses and construct large panel data sets. Within a given country, local jurisdictions are typically subject to the same set of rules and are characterized by a relative cultural, legal, and constitutional homogeneity. Exploiting the coexistence of institutional homogeneity and (hopefully sufficient) heterogeneity of outcomes and economic conditions allows researchers to explore how accountability plays out in the field. The main task for researchers is then to find either particular institutional features (e.g., term limits) or implementation of reforms (introduction of new local taxes or random audits) that may allow one to identify causal effects in a robust way. On the one hand, these studies can use very sharp identification strategies and offer readers with convincing causal explanations; on the other hand, they often lack in external validity, as they are bound to speak naturally only to the country that is object of the study, or even more stringently to the regression subsample. Some studies focus on particular institutional features or issues, such as term limits, the introduction of particular taxes, and the relevance of neighbors' policy choices in fostering accountability; other studies delve further into this by exploring the role that media penetration and cultural factors such as the level of social capital play in shaping voters' ability to hold politicians into account. Finally, we also review studies on local government bailouts and soft budget constraints; this limited number of studies seeks to find empirical backing to a fairly simple theoretical concept, tightly knit with the very existence of a federal structure. Local governments may not fully internalize the cost of incurring into debt, as they may hold an expectation that in case of financial trouble the central government may bail them out. We will explore how empirical research has tried to find credible empirical proxies for the local government expectations of bailout and measure this phenomenon. This section will start from this latter class of papers, and later sections will then go back to cross-country analyses on decentralization and accountability.

Many countries in the world have regulations about term limits; they are imposed on very high offices such as those of the presidents of the United States and of France, down to mayors of small villages in Italy and Brazil. A term-limit regulation typically bars incumbent politicians who served two consecutive terms in office from running for reelection; more rarely, these limits bar politicians who served only one term or another set number of terms. The availability of large panel of electoral data in local or federated governments makes this issue very popular in empirical fiscal federalism. The effect on government accountability is treated by many authors, starting from Besley and Case (1995a), who also offer a theoretical underpinning based on a political agency model. The central issue is that term-limited politicians lack reelection incentives, and this fundamentally affects both their policy choices and voters' choices on whether to reelect first-term incumbents or not. Voting allows citizens to select politicians according to ability or consonance with respect to their own preferences; electoral incentives push incumbent politicians to deliver policies that are more consonant with voters. The theoretical intuition is that the principal-agent relationship between voters and politicians is bound to be less effective when the agent lacks the incentive to behave in a consonant fashion. The expectation is therefore that a second-term politician will exert less effort, and voters will be more likely to reelect politicians who deliver higher payoffs to voters in their first term. Besley and Case's (1995a) empirical analysis relies on data from US gubernatorial elections from 1950 to 1986. This period is particularly apt for studying the effect of term limits as state policies on governors' term limit has been very heterogeneous across time and space: the data set includes states with no, one-term and two-term limits and a number of states changing their stance within the sample period (typically introducing term limits). This time- and cross-section variability is of major help in constructing a tight identification strategy, allowing the use of state and time fixed effects. For example, simply comparing first- and second-term governors would be problematic: as second-term governors have gone twice through electoral scrutiny, have "by construction" more experience, they may be higher quality, or they may be more entrenched with lobbies and the bureaucracy. Having states reforming their term-limit policies allows the disentangling of term-limit effects from second-term effect. The results show that term-limited governors, because of their lack of electoral incentives, enforce policies that are less popular and less liked by voters: they levy higher sales and income taxes and have higher expenditure. These results are driven by Democratic governors, while no statistically significant effect is found for Republican ones. Republican governors instead are found to lower the state minimum wage when they are subject to term limits. In this sense it seems uncontroversial that term limits generate inefficiencies, eliciting a term-based taxation cycle and increasing the overall deadweight loss of taxation. There is thus prima facie evidence that term limits may be detrimental for voters' welfare. This somehow clashes with the observation that more and more legislations have decided to adopt them.

In the same spirit, Lowry, Alt, and Ferree (1998) use a very similar data set to explore another channel through which accountability may be affected. Their work exploits the institutional homogeneity across US states, too, in order to test the effect of having a divided government (i.e., situations in which the governor and the legislature are ideologically nonconsonant). The voters' inference problem following a divided government period is more complicated, making it more challenging for the principal (voters) to select and control the agent (the politician); this, in turn, allows the agent to engage in moral hazard relatively more. Term limits still play an important role in the identification strategy, with term-limited governors serving as an (imperfect) control group and non-term-limited governors as a treatment group, fully subjected to reelection incentives. The authors calculate fiscal "surprises" (i.e., changes in revenues, taxation, or deficit) with respect to the trend. The main thrust of the paper is that voters are better able to hold politicians into account when they can easily attribute the responsibility of fiscal policy to them. This is the case for gubernatorial as opposed to legislative elections (where it is the whole chamber and not the single representative who is co-responsible for policies), and for cases of unified as opposed to divided governments. Moreover – which is of less interest for us – voters' expectations on policy are party-dependent: voters will reward Republican politicians for cutting taxes and Democratic politicians for increasing spending. The identification strategy relies on the richness of the data set, with heterogeneous term-limit rules across states and time and good variability in the ideological leaning of governors and legislatures, but does not fully address issues such as reverse causality and endogeneity. This is true because voting behavior – and therefore partisanship of governor and legislature – may be affecting fiscal policy, but also because the use of term-limited and non-term-limited governors is a risky strategy, as second-term governors are a self-selected subset of first-term governors, who are very likely to have different unobservables than the universe of first-term incumbents.

This issue is addressed and overcome by Alt, Bueno de Mesquita, and Rose (2011), who try to look further into the effects of term limits parsing between the effect of electoral incentives (or lack of thereof) and experience. Term-limited governors are often second-term governors, who have spent four years learning how the government machine works, and that have survived twice the electoral selection process. Comparing same-term governors, they find that term-limited ones are *more* profligate, showing that the lack of electoral incentives lowers the quality of policy and the accountability to voters. Similarly, they find that holding term-limit status constant, governors with more experience (second-term governors) are *less* profligate, evidencing a competence (or selection) effect. These results highlight very clearly the positive role of electoral incentives both in terms of disciplining and selecting politicians, and how term limits break this mechanism generating lower quality policies in lame-duck terms. The results once again heavily rely on the heterogeneity and time variability of term-limit arrangements in US gubernatorial elections. This identification strategy is surely robust, especially considering that results hold also when discarding governors directly affected by changes in term-limit policy, as this may have been endogenously decided by them. The only caveat is that one has to accept that the change in term-limit does not change the average quality of the pool of candidates (i.e., assuming that moving from one- to two-term limits does not encourage marginally better candidates to run). All in all, this contribution is the most accurate and robust description on the positive effects of tenure and the negative effects of term limits on policy outcomes and politicians' accountability.

Leaving US governors aside, Klein and Sakurai (2015) construct a data set of about 3,000 Brazilian municipalities in the 2000s. They explore in particular the combined effect of political budget cycle and term limits. They compare the end-of-term fiscal choices of term-limited and non-term-limited mayors. As elections approaches, reelection seeking mayors are found to move spending from current expenditure (such as personnel) to capital investments (such as new buses, schools or infrastructure), as these spending items are believed to be more visible and pay off more in terms of votes. This end-of-term behavior is not detected instead in term-limited mayors. Unlike in the US governors' case, Brazilian mayors are subject to two-term limit throughout the sample period, so the authors can only argue that what is observed is not simply a "second-term" effect (e.g., for the increased experience and selectedness of these mayors), as opposed to a "term-limit effect." Concerns for endogeneity of fiscal policy and voting behavior are addressed using a System-GMM technique, where the lagged dependent variables are used as instruments of the (differenced) lagged dependent variables.

Italy introduced a two-term limit for (newly) elected mayors in 1993. This has been exploited by Coviello and Gagliarducci (2017), who exploit the fact that this reform created two groups of mayors elected within a few months of each other (just before and just after the reform), but with different constraints in terms of term limits. As first- and second-term mayors have different characteristics and cannot be used as a treatment and control groups, the authors rely on a quasi-experimental technique to address this issue. Through a regression discontinuity design (RDD; see, for example, Calonico et al., 2019), they compare municipalities where the first-term mayor nearly won or nearly lost. Mayors who barely win and their electoral opponents are bound to be on average very similar on unobservable and observable qualities, differing only in tenure. This deals with the fact that (possibly) mayors with longer tenure may have been reelected also thanks to their particular behavior (e.g., using their power to favor local bidders in local procurement auctions) or ability. This paper is particularly innovative also in terms of the dependent variable they use: they obtain data on public procurement auctions and find that public procurement auctions in localities ruled by more experienced mayors (mayors with more terms of tenure) are more likely to have fewer bidders and lower discounts, giving more than suggestive evidence that tenure in office increases entrenchment and the chance of corruption. This is firsthand evidence that term limits may be serving a positive purpose, reducing the likelihood of entrenchment and collusion with local contractors, and that accountability may be decaying over time as incumbency advantage lowers the bar for incumbent mayors.

Aragón and Pique (2020) rely as well on a regression discontinuity design, looking into data from municipalities in Peru and concentrating their attention on close elections, in which (re-)election can be considered as good as random.

As Peru lacks a term-limit rule, the difference between first- and second-term mayor is purely driven by experience or selection. Focusing on close races, and looking at taxation, current, and capital spending, they find no significant difference between first- and second-term mayors. The "symmetry" of electoral incentives across terms makes the mayors' policies undistinguishable across terms. This paper, of course, is unable to investigate whether the detrimental effects of tenure, such as increased corruption, collusion, and entrenchment may be present.

De Janvy, Finan, and Saboulet (2012) also examine the effect of term limits on accountability, using a very innovative proxy for performance. They take data from a conditional cash transfer (CCT) program in Brazil aimed at reducing school dropout rates for poor households. Their data set is extensive, with more than 200,000 students' outcomes, in about 250 municipalities. As noted previously, Brazilian mayors are subject to a two-term limit; this paper's identification strategy compares the CCT outcomes in municipalities with mayors in their first term – therefore seeking reelection – with mayors in their second term, and therefore barred from seeking reelection. Their result is that the success of this program was mainly driven by first-term mayors, while second-term mayor saw little to no effect in terms of improvement of dropout rates. As already seen, comparing first- and second-term mayors is problematic, as they may be incomparable groups: reelection may be a sign of higher quality or ability of the incumbent mayor. This is confirmed by the fact that first-term mayors who performed better (in the top quartile of the CCT performance ranking) were more likely to be reelected. The authors address this issue by also looking into the subset of first-term mayors who then managed to be reelected, and that therefore should have comparable unobserved characteristics.

Bordignon, Gamalerio, and Turati (2013) shed light on one of the possible mechanisms that may be driving the electoral accountability. Using a panel data set of Italian mayoral elections and municipal budgets, they explore the effect of vertical fiscal gap on electoral outcomes. We already reviewed evidence of the elections allowing voters to hold politicians into account and limiting moral hazard: in the absence of electoral incentives (as in the case of term limits), public policy outcomes worsen. The intuition behind Bordignon, Gamalerio, and Turati (2013) is that municipalities which are highly reliant on external funding as opposed to own revenues face a similar challenge. In other words, higher fiscal gaps (higher reliance on grants from upper-tier governments) lower the incentives for voters to select high-quality mayors. Their paper goes further into distinguishing between mayors with "managerial ability," who are preferred by voters in localities highly reliant on own revenues, and mayors with "political experience," who are more useful in localities where lobbying with higher tier politicians is necessary to obtain grants, and are preferred by voters in localities highly reliant on them. The paper exploits the 1993 introduction of a property tax (ICI) that increased the fiscal autonomy of municipalities in a highly heterogeneous way, depending on the stock of housing and of its land-registry value. As land registry values are seldom updated, this is only loosely linked with the actual value of the stock of housing. This feature addresses the problem of endogeneity, together with an instrumental variable technique in which VAT revenues at the provincial level are used as an indicator of local fiscal capacity. The sample size is quite small, concentrating on about ninety major Italian cities for which data are available. Measurement of political and managerial skills is also imperfect, with the first proxied by years of experience in political office and the second proxied by education and profession. This paper is particularly interesting also with respect to the role of social capital and other "cultural" variables: including social capital proxies as controls does not affect their results. In short, both *culture* and *incentives* matter in shaping accountability. More generally, this paper highlights how voters' incentive to hold politicians into account are larger the more local governments are relying on locally raised funds.

Finally, Revelli (2016a) explores the impact of an important and often overlooked determinant of the actual degree of fiscal decentralization in multi-tiered government structures – the extent and intensity of tax and expenditure limitations that upper-tier authorities impose onto lower-tier ones – on the functioning of the local democratic process in terms of voter turnout, political competition, and candidate selection. Indeed, the conventional rational voting framework suggests that fiscal decentralization should foster voter turnout and party competition in local elections by raising their stakes (Andersen, Fiva and Natvik, 2014). On the other hand, its impact on the mechanism of candidate selection is less obvious. Within the most general model of voluntary costly voting where ideologically biased voters (say, conservative versus progressive) receive informative signals about candidates' quality (commonly valued competence), any mechanism narrowing the positional issue gap between candidates makes it more likely that voting occurs according to competence signals than to voters' ideological views. This has two key implications. First, by deemphasizing positional/ideological issues, top-down fiscal limitations make it more likely that voting in local elections occurs according to common values (signals about the competence of candidates) than to private values (ideological views), with such switch lowering voter turnout owing to the perception of smaller electoral stakes. Second, such a switch improves the selection property of local elections by favoring the convergence of votes to the most valent candidate, irrespective of their ideologies. The empirical analysis employs a difference-in-differences research design that exploits changes in state tax limits having heterogeneous impact on more than 7,000 Italian local authorities during the 2000s, finding that tax limits provoke a moderate reduction in voter turnout and candidate competition, some improvement in proxies of candidate valence, and a sizeable rise in elected mayors' win margins. The evidence is compatible with the hypothesis that by lessening the ideological stakes of local elections, tax limits favor voters' party-line crossing and convergence of votes to the most valent candidates.

6 Transparency, Information, and Social Capital

The papers reviewed in the previous section highlighted the intimate link between elections and accountability. Another highly salient issue that helps voters hold politicians accountable is information: voters will vote according to the information they have available, and more efficient political systems will see a better flow of information between politicians and voters. Similarly, lower-quality politicians will be happy to have less transparent polities and are more likely to thrive in localities where media diffusion and newspaper readership are lower. Both information diffusion and media penetration are highly correlated with the level of social capital. Social capital is a multidimensional concept, broadly defined as "trust, norms and network" (Putnam 1993), which helps societies overcome free riding and foster cooperation, with the idea that "trust and norms of civic cooperation are essential to well-functioning societies, and to the economic progress of these societies" (Knack and Keefer, 1997). Of course, this concept is highly endogenous; Putnam (1993) himself points out how decentralization may foster social capital, encouraging community participation. At the same time, central governments may be more prone to decentralize to localities that show high levels of cooperation and citizens' involvement.

A number of contributions attempt to explore these issues in decentralized systems. Besley and Burgess (2002) use data from 16 Indian states for more than 30 years (1958–1992) to test voters' responsiveness to policies. They explore the issue of accountability leveraging in particular on two data sources: first, India has a substantially free press, with large time and space variation in its penetration and readership that also includes the poorer strata of society; second, they use the detailed records of relief and natural disaster spending by state governments. The latter gives the advantage of providing information linked to not only largely exogenous shocks such as drought or floods, but also highly visible spending items by a large fraction of the voting population. As newspaper circulation may be endogenous, it is also instrumented with media ownership data at the local level. The authors find that political competition – as proxied by seat margin of the ruling party at the state level – and election timing does affect spending decisions. In particular, it affects food distribution programs but not disaster relief spending; the authors argue that this difference may be to the higher visibility of the former with respect to the latter. Most interestingly, policy responsiveness is strongly linked with newspaper readership, which amplifies the governors' response to calamities or food shortages. It is quite sizeable, as responsiveness more than doubles, passing from the median to the 75th percentile in media diffusion.

Using a completely different approach, Alt, Dryer-Lassen, and Skilling (2002) investigate the channels of accountability in an uncommon way. They collect data on the fiscal transparency of US states; the measurement of transparency is based on a number of items, such as whether shared accounting practices are followed, whether annual budgets are regularly made public, whether the governor or legislature can pass open-ended spending programs, and so on. They look into whether transparency has an effect on the governor's approval rating, calculated as an average over the years 1986–1995. This is just for a single cross-section of US states, which implies that the number of observations is very limited and there is little space (or attempt) to deal with endogeneity. The results are robust to various tweaks of the fiscal transparency index and point to a solid correlation between transparency and approval rating for the incumbent governor. Given the research question, the possible endogeneity of fiscal transparency remains the main issue. The authors interpret the results as evidence that transparency enhances accountability, and therefore disciplines incumbents, who in turn behave in a more consonant way. This is certainly a possible explanation, but more research is needed to establish something more than a conditional correlation and explore the transmission mechanism.

Extending the previous work, Alt, Dryer-Lassen, and Rose (2006) also look into the determinants of fiscal transparency in US states. They expand the methodology used by Alt, Dryer-Lassen, and Skilling (2002) to code transparency practices and make it into a 30-year-long data set (1972–2002). The main theoretical background to this paper is that the political agency problem of voters, who try to limit politician's moral hazard and select effectively the best candidates, is bound to work better when voters are given better information: transparency in fiscal policy can improve accountability and selection. The direction of causality is not obvious, though, as better politicians may be more prone to increase transparency. The aim of this paper is to see whether the choice on the level of transparency of each state is affected by political variables, and in particular by political competition. This is proxied by variables such as a "divided government" dummy and measures of political competition in gubernatorial and state legislature elections. The panel structure of the data set allows for the inclusion of state fixed effects. In the basic OLS specification, they find that both political competition (whether in legislative or gubernatorial elections) and divided government are correlated with higher transparency. These results remain solidly in the realm of conditional correlations, as no further investigation is done into the causality of this relationship. The highly endogenous choice of political competition and the difficulty in finding a good quality instrument do not allow for further explorations.

Ferraz and Finan (2008) exploit a policy of random audits of Brazilian municipalities implemented by the federal government. An extensive audit program was carried out in the years around the 2004 municipal election round, allowing researchers to separate the universe of municipalities going to elections in a treatment (audited) and control (not audited, or not yet audited). Some of the audits resulted in criminal or administrative charges being made. This paper is also able to measure whether the effect of these random audits on voting behavior is affected by the presence of media, measuring the penetration of local radio stations. All in all, this audit policy enforced by the Brazilian federal government on municipalities allows to explore a number of interesting issues on to do with political accountability. They are able to see whether the audits per se have an effect, whether the amount of misgivings exposed by the audit matters, whether corrupt politicians (who would be exposed after the elections) suffer as well in elections. Finally, using radio penetration data, the authors are able to look into the transmission mechanism – in other words, whether radio stations and media in general can be seen as a vehicle for enhanced transparency and accountability. The random design of these audits allows the researchers to establish robust causal links with no need to use other techniques than simple OLS regressions. The results are very clear cut: audits affect reelection chances only as long as they uncover corrupt or irregular behaviors; this effect is also strongly correlated with the *amount* of corruption exposed (number of violations found in the report), while post-election audits have no significant effect, even if they discover irregularities. In other words, the uncovering of misbehaviors through audits negatively hits reelection chances of incumbents, revealing new valuable information to voters. The presence of local radio stations magnifies these effects, with the likelihood of reelection decreasing by 3.7% where there is no radio station and by 16.1% where radio stations are present. These results very clearly highlight both voters' willingness to hold politicians into account when relevant information reaches them and the importance of having efficient channels for this information to be diffused, such as a lively media environment.

Costas-Pérez, Solé-Ollé, and Sorribas-Navarro (2012) also highlight the link between local government accountability, corruption scandals, and media penetration, with data from Spanish municipal elections and budgets. They cover a period characterized by the real estate bubble, in which the bulk of corrupted practices in Spanish municipalities accounted to bribery cases related with planning permissions. They use an extensive database of corruption cases compiled by a think tank, based on news stories in local and national media outlets. This think tank, albeit with a clear ideological stance, appears to have collected unbiased information on scandals. The authors integrated this data set with targeted news searches, to cover the period between 1995 and 2007, covering three municipal legislatures, and then focused on corruption scandals hitting incumbent politicians at the time of the news story (hence excluding politicians who were already out of office for any other motive). The identification strategy relies on comparing municipalities experiencing a scandal for the first time with municipalities that did not experience a scandal in the previous municipal legislature. The regression sample accounts for more than 4,000 observations, of which just beyond 200 are from the treatment group. The results highlight how voters punish incumbents who have been found corrupt by news media. Voting behavior appears to be quite sophisticated, with voters punishing politicians when accusations were not minor and rewarding politicians who were acquitted or for which no charge followed from the initial accusations. The authors also detect a differentiated effect according to the timing of these accusations within the electoral cycle, with electoral effects being amplified if the news story happened in the second half of the term. These results once again highlight not only the fact that voters hold politicians into account, but that media and the information they diffuse are instrumental in amplifying the channels through which accountability works.

Fernandez-Vasquez, Barberà, and Rivero (2016) explore a further issue related to accountability. We saw a number of contributions highlighting how voters punish corruption, which is especially true when media outlets diffuse information about it. This paper looks into whether voters are more lenient (or accepting) when corruption scandals highlight illegal activities which may have positive economic spillover to their locality. For example, increasing the housing stock may benefit local population, even if this was done damaging a protected area, while over-invoicing in public procurement is advantageous only to the seller involved. The authors collected an extensive data set of corruption scandals involving Spanish mayors, coded these scandals according to whether the crime involved was bound to be positive for the local economy or not, and looked into whether these had any effect on electoral outcomes, as measured by the vote share of the current incumbent. They look into the cross section of municipal elections in 2011 (and the previous round, to calculate the variation in votes for the incumbent) and corruption episodes uncovered during the 2007–2011 municipal legislature. A total of 75 corruption cases were uncovered, 29 of which were coded as generating economic benefits for the local economy. As these scandals can be treated as exogenous, the identification strategy need not rely on anything more sophisticated than simple OLS. This paper highlights once more the role of the press in diffusing information on corruption scandal and the role that elections play in holding politicians into account. It adds, though, a further layer, pointing out that voters may not be sensitive to any type of corruption, or better – that they may punish corruption as long as they think that this is welfare decreasing for their community.

Transparency and accountability are at the center of Bordignon, Grembi, and Piazza's (2017) contribution, which exploits the introduction of a new local tax characterized by a lower level of transparency. They build a data set of Italian municipal elections and public finance. Municipal government own revenues were mostly reliant on a highly salient property tax (on this, see also the already cited Bracco et al., 2015). From 1999 onward, municipalities have been allowed to impose a personal income tax surcharge, which is instead considered less salient, as it is paid together with the overall income tax liability to the national government, which will then distribute the surcharge revenues to municipalities. The change may be considered exogenous from the point of view of municipal governments, allowing the authors to check the characteristics of the mayors who have used more extensively this additional revenue source. They find that mayors who had been elected with smaller margin of victory, who were not term limited and in municipalities with lower levels of social capital were more prone to use this revenue source. The exogeneity of the reform allows the authors to claim a causal link between electoral incentives and transparency of fiscal choices, as revealed by the choice of revenue mix. The paper highlights a number of interesting features: electoral accountability can be hindered or enhanced by the politician's choices, and politicians will have stronger incentives to reduce transparency (and therefore accountability) with stronger reelectoral incentives. This license that politicians enjoy is limited by the capacity of voters to read public policy and hold them into account, as proxied by the level of social capital. From the policy perspective, it appears evident how accountability is enhanced by the ability of voters to attribute specific tax liabilities to the authority levying the tax.

Finally, it is worth looking into Klašnja's (2015) work. This work explores the potentially negative effect of tenure using a data set of Romanian mayors. To our knowledge, this – together with Coviello and Gagliarducci (2017) – is one of the few papers explicitly motivating the introduction of term limits with strong empirical evidence. The reason many countries introduced term limits is that even if they lower the disciplining effect of electoral incentives and foster the chances of moral hazard, they protect against entrenchment of politicians and collusion with the administration or particular interested parties. This paper chases exactly this intuition, arguing that as tenure increases, the chances a politician engages in corrupt practices increase. He draws on a data set of three rounds of elections of the 3,000 Romanian municipalities, using a Regression Discontinuity Design to isolate incumbency in a quasi-experimental fashion. The author also constructs a very rich measure of municipality-level corruption, including measures of mayors' wealth accumulation and indices of transparency of procurement procedures at the local level. Finally, this paper exploits a discontinuity in mayoral salary according to a population threshold, arguing that the incentives to engage in corruption decrease as the mayoral salary increases. The combined use of all of these quasi-experimental designs affords the author a very sharp and robust identification strategy. The results highlight that in Romania there is indeed an incumbency disadvantage in mayoral elections, with the probability of reelection being half for incumbents. The paper also establishes that corruption is more rampant as mayoral salary decreases. Exploiting these two findings, the paper also shows that the incumbency disadvantage is not significant in localities with higher mayoral salary, while it is very large and statistically significant in localities with smaller mayoral salary. Combining regression discontinuities both at the population (and therefore mayoral salary) and margin of victory level, these results are deemed to causally isolate the effect of corruption on incumbency (dis)advantage. All in all, this paper is proving very sharply that corruption increases with tenure, especially for those mayors who have stronger incentives to seek some "extra cash." As many of these country-based studies, and especially using a technique such as RDD, the issue of external validity is very salient: it is difficult to say if these results may be generalizable to the universe of Romanian municipalities, let alone to localities beyond Romania. The calculation of ad hoc local indices of corruption is nevertheless a very rare thing to observe, which may be exploited creatively also in other countries and other contexts.

The last two contributions pointing out to a link between "good" government outcome and voters' information focus not so much on the media as a means of information diffusion but on the effect of grassroots involvement in local governments as an enhancer of electoral accountability. Geys, Heinemann, and Kalb (2010) look at a sample of about one thousand municipal budgets and three rounds of mayoral elections in Baden-Wurttemberg, a German federal state. In particular, after estimating the efficiency frontier through stochastic frontier analysis, they explore its link with a wide array of measures of voters' involvement. Their hypothesis is that voters' involvement improves efficiency (as it improves accountability, reduces moral hazard, and improves electoral selection and self-selection into candidacy), and that this is especially true when fiscal autonomy is higher (i.e., vertical fiscal gaps are lower). Voter involvement is measured first and foremost by electoral turnout, which is a rather coarse measure, but also through slightly more sophisticated measures, such as the existence of grassroot voters' associations or the share of eligible voters across residents. Their outcomes are first related to the calculations of efficiency. Political competition is positively correlated with local government efficiency. The mechanism is not explored, and causality is far from established, but this is still a relevant finding that goes in the same direction of other papers' findings. The three measures of voters' involvement have positive and significant effect on efficiency, too, with this result being driven mostly by more fiscally autonomous municipalities. This is most coherent with explanations relying on agency theory: voters are able and are incentivized to hold politicians into account the more they see the link between taxes and public good provisions and are able to act consequently in elections. This paper does not push for a causal interpretation; the results may be interpreted as simple conditional correlations, which corroborate similar evidence from other works reviewed in this section.

With Goncalves (2014), we turn back to Brazilian municipalities, and to another peculiar feature of their governance. Using a data set of municipal budgets between 1990 and 2004, the author explores the effect of "participatory budgets" on public good provision and expenditure patterns. The participatory budgets are a novel way of deciding how to allocate expenditures through grassroot citizens involvement, implemented through neighborhood assemblies and informally elected representatives. This practice was started by the Brazilian Workers Party in the eighties and followed up by other (mostly left-wing) mayors. All in all, a couple of hundred of municipalities decided to adopt them, out of a universe of more than 5,000. The author finds that municipalities adopting these budgets spend more on expenditure items such as health or sanitation and have better health-related outcomes (e.g., lower child mortality rates). This contribution is particularly interesting, as it points to the fact that greater citizens' involvement is correlated with better public good provision and better outcomes. This close link that decentralized governments can establish between administration and population, between revenue collection and spending, seems to be key in guaranteeing an accountable public good provision mechanism. At the same time, the results just mentioned are plagued by endogeneity: the subset of municipalities deciding to adopt these participatory budgets are not a random selection; they are politically left-leaning and are likely to be places with already important levels of participation. The simultaneity of participatory budget and good government is partially addressed by restricting the sample to those municipality that adopt participatory budgets at some point in time, and relying on within-municipality time variation, and also by a matching technique. All in all, though, the worries about endogeneity are not fully dispelled.

7 Soft Budget Constraints

Another important issue related to the information flow within jurisdictions has to do with the so-called soft budget constraint (SBC). This concept has been pioneered by Kornai (1986) and reviewed a number of times (see, for example, Maskin, 1999, and Kornai, Maskin, and Roland, 2003, who applied it to state-owned enterprises within planned economies). The government may have political and occupational interest in keeping a firm afloat independently of its economic viability; at the same time, the firm's management anticipates this and has lower incentives to be efficient. In the end, firms end up with higher levels of debt, in expectation of a government bailout in case of troubles. This lead to the idea that these firms' budget constraint was "soft" in view of the expectation of further transfer. This concept has been extensively applied also in the context of fiscal federalism. There are many reasons why a local government may incur in extra expenditures (or debt) in expectation of a central government bailout: first of all, shared political allegiance between local and central government may make it politically and electorally convenient to grant extra resources; moreover, local government may be providing essential public services such as health care, and it may not be legally, constitutionally, or politically viable for them to cut expenditure and reduce their public good provision. The idea of the soft budget constraint is somehow related to the already cited "flypaper effect" (see Section 2 of this Element), which highlights how an increase in grants stimulates increases in public spending that are larger than an equivalent increase in local income. Under the soft budget constraint setup, the local government becomes first mover by being profligate (e.g., running a deficit) *in expectation* of a bailout from the central government. Local government's bailout expectations play a central role, making empirical research quite difficult. It is challenging to find credible empirical proxies for expectations of bailout. Researchers had to parse between situations of an increase in expenditures caused by a bailout expectation (soft budget constraint), from a number of other situations, which may be observationally equivalent: the "simple" smoothing of expenditure caused by an expectation of an increase in grants (e.g., because of a general increase in government expenditure), economic shocks, yardstick competition, and politically motivated grant policies.

Bordignon and Turati (2009) find that regions in Italy that had lower expectations of being bailed out by the central government were more prone to restructure their expenditure in correspondence of the new fiscal targets of the Maastricht Treaty. As argued by Wildasin (1997), local governments, especially when they provide health care as in the case of Italy, can hardly be allowed to fail by the central government. To proxy for bailout expectations, the paper exploits the budget tightening elicited by the race to the euro and the Maastricht Treaty parameter in the nineties, together with the variation in time and amount of ex post bailing out of the regional health care deficits. More specifically, the change in bailing-out expectation is proxied in various ways: through a "euro" dummy, pinpointing the time of fiscal restraint that came before 1997, leading up to the decision on which countries were allowed to join the EU; an index of public tightness (the ratio between Italian and average EU deficit); political alignment between regional and central government; and a number of variables proxying for regional fiscal capacity and autonomy. These variables are used both in their own right as proxy for the bailout expectation, and as an instrument in estimating the causes of expenditure decision by regional governments. They find that central government funding is affected by these variables, and as these variables proxy bailout expectations, regional government expenditures are also affected by them.

Crivelli, Leive, and Stratmann (2010) take a different avenue, looking at a cross-country evidence of soft budget constraints with a data set of 25 OECD countries between 1990 and 2007. They use a measure of vertical fiscal gap and a number of variables describing limitations to create debt for local governments based on questionnaires of government officials to proxy the presence of a soft budget constraint. The authors argue that as the central government cannot credibly commit to not bailing out local government on health care expenditure; these measures are a good proxy of bailout expectations. This cross-country analysis does find that health care expenditure is positively correlated with these measures of budget "softness"; in particular, vertical fiscal gaps have strong effects on health care spending in countries where borrowing autonomy is higher. These results are robust, but they remained plagued by a fundamental problem: what they measure is not so much the expectation of future bailouts but the possibility to spend beyond one's own present resources, either through borrowing or through receiving grants. As described in Sections 2.2 and 2.4 of this Element, they may just highlight the lack of accountability linked with expenditure decentralization when not coupled with fiscal decentralization.

Thanks to a peculiarity of the Swedish grant system, Pettersson-Lidbom (2011) is able to model with much higher precision the expectation of bailout. Sweden passed from a fairly loose system of intergovernmental grants in the 1980s, when a subset of the 300 localities were bailed out a total of 1408 times, to a formula-based one. This new system was put in place also to affect localities' bailout expectation and "harden" their budget constraint. Nevertheless, some localities still went in financial distress, and at the end of the 1990s, some of them where bailed out by the central government. The actual (future) occurrence of bailouts and a number of other variables such as political alignment with central government are used to proxy the *expectation* of bailout by local governments. As future bailout may be endogenous to current debt decisions, this measure is instrumented with the occurrence of (future) bailouts to neighboring localities; this sharp identification strategy allows causal interpretation of the results: the author does find that debt levels are caused by the expectation of bailouts.

Sorribas-Navarro (2011) takes once again a different outlook on this issue: rather than exploring spending behavior of local governments, they look into the bailout decision of central government through both discretionary and non-discretionary grants. In short, they estimate whether current grants are determined by past level of debts of local government, after controlling for a number of economic and political control variables. To avoid endogeneity, local debt levels are instrumented with variables related to changes in interest rates and to the structure of regional debt stock. The results highlight that the central government does bailout local government as they incur in higher debt. This paper, however, does not go into modeling the expenditure (and debt) behavior by local governments: in other words, we do not know whether Spanish localities incur more debt as they expect to be bailed out in the future, but we do know that the central government bails out local government that overspent.

Baskaran (2012) tests for soft budget constraint on German data from 1975 to 2005, exploiting the intuition that bailout expectations should be related (1) in a positive way, to the availability of central government funds, which are in turn negatively related to the central government borrowing pattern (2) in a negative way, to the amount of resources already granted to other localities. The identification strategy relies on checking whether (federal) states deficits are affected by these horizontal and vertical interactions – that is, by the neighbors' and federal deficits. An instrumental variable approach is used to bypass the endogeneity problem, using other states' lagged weighted average deficit to GDP ratio and their weighted average contemporaneous population growth and federal government ideology and federal election dummies as instruments for the deficit to GDP ratio of the federal government. Through this, the author is able to detect a presence of SBC, as highlighted by strong horizontal inter-actions: jurisdictions incur in larger deficits as the central government becomes more generous to neighboring jurisdiction, contributing to a sort of upward ratchet effect in local spending.

Dietrichson and Ellegård (2015) and Ben-Bassat, Dahan, and Klor (2016) explore how to mitigate the SBC problem with Swedish and Israeli data. They both highlight that bailouts per se need not increase the expectations of bailouts and fiscal indiscipline, as long as the central government commitment to a "hardening" of the budget constraint is credible. This happened in both countries through provisions such as a credible conditionality program in Sweden (in the former contribution) or a government appointed accountant that checks on the locality's financial decision (as in the latter contribution). All in all, it is striking how only Pettersson-Lidbom (2011) seem to find a fully credible way to empirically proxy for bailout expectations, using a long data set of *actual* occurrences of bailouts. More generally, the few authors who attempted to detect patterns of SBC used very different identification strategies and techniques, highlighting how difficult it is to find credible empirical proxies for the expectation of future bailouts.

8 Cross-Country Studies on Decentralization

Many cross-country studies try to establish a link between decentralization and some measurable outcomes related to accountability and responsiveness to voters' preferences. For a number of reasons, several of these studies focus on corruption: independently of the institutional setup, it is generally recognized that corruption induces an unfair and wasteful distribution of resources and hinders economic development;[13] in addition, there is reasonably good inter-nationally comparable data on the level of corruption.

From the theoretical perspective, it is unclear whether decentralization is linked to (or causes) corruption. As already mentioned, Weingast (1995) and Seabright (1996) note that the smaller distance between voters and local politi-cians may give voters more scope for exit or voice and simplify the monitoring task, while Prud'homme (1995) argues that the judiciary may be more effective in controlling central government agencies. Also, capture by interest groups may be easier at the local level (Shleifer and Vishny, 1993; Bardhan and Mookherjee, 2000), and local politicians may hold a stronger monopoly power over voters (Kunicová and Rose-Ackerman, 2005). Reliable measures and a credible identification strategy are the main challenges for this strand of

---

[13] Baskaran, Feld, and Schnellenbach (2016) provide an excellent theoretical and empirical review and a meta-analysis of the estimated effects of fiscal decentralization on economic growth.

literature, which mostly struggles to find tight identification strategies that go beyond conditional correlations and to find suitable measures of comparable information across time and space.

The first study to address this issue is Treisman (2000). This is a wide-ranging work that digs into the causes of corruption. It uses some of the most common measures of corruption – that is, those produced regularly by Transparency International (TI). This is a composite index constructed through aggregating a number of different polls of local interested parties such as local leaders and businessmen, but also polling external "experts." This is a well-established index, calculated with regularity and considered highly reliable, but is subject to a common pitfall: it mostly relies on the informed opinions and perceptions of a sample of interested parties. In other words, it is closer to a measure of the *perception* of corruption, rather than a measure of corruption itself. The various components of the index appear to be highly correlated with each other and quite stable across time, reassuring substantially about their reliability. Moreover, it is also highly correlated with other independently calculated indices, such as the International Country Risk Guide. All of this should reassure readers on the fact that this index is sound and that different sources have highly correlated perceptions on the level of corruption in a country. This does not necessarily imply that these perceptions are not biased. The reliability of cross-country corruption measures remains an issue. To address this, Treisman (2000) also applies a WLS specification, underweighting those countries whose TI index components show a higher variance, indicating a larger uncertainty of operators on the level of corruption of that country.

As for decentralization, Treisman (2000) uses a formal (or de jure) definition, looking at whether there is more than a tier of government, and if decentralized governments have any specific task, autonomy, or constitutional protection. The main problem with such a measure is the distance one might observe between the constitutional provision and the actual practice in terms of public goods delivery or local government autonomy in setting public policy. The analysis focuses on a single cross-section of 64 developed and developing countries. Corruption is found to be higher in federal countries, and this is especially true for the least developed (non-OECD) ones. The study controls for many factors that may correlate with decentralization, such as land area and ethnic fractionalization, in the attempt to address the problems of endogeneity, reverse causality, or omitted variable bias. However, the small sample size does not allow robustness checks – for instance, if the results are affected by dropping single or group of observations from the regressions and no other attempt is made to address the simultaneity between decentralization and corruption.

Fisman and Gatti (2002) perform a similar analysis, focusing on the effect of fiscal rather than political decentralization, finding opposite results: fiscal decentralization is robustly correlated with lower levels of corruption. This result is probably highly dependent on the different measure of decentralization they use: this work relies on IMF measurements of share of decentralized expenditure and revenues. This measure is likely to catch how much "work" is effectively carried out by local government, independently of whether the institutional form chosen by the country is more or less federal. They also add as a regressor a dummy variable for (institutionally) federal countries, which appears not to be significant. As a measure of corruption, they use the already mentioned ICRG measure of corruption, which is again a survey-based measure focused on assessing the likelihood that a public official may solicit a bribe payment. The sample size is relatively small, at about 60 observations. Endogeneity is addressed through a two-stage least squares analysis, instrumenting decentralization with a number of dummy variables defining a country's legal system. The validity of the instrument critically hinges on the argument that the legal system affects a country's level of corruption only through decentralization, which remains still open to debate.

Also Gerring and Thacker (2004) find that decentralization is correlated with increased corruption, defining decentralization through a composite index of – among other things – existing IMF statistics and a constitution-based index of unitarianism. With a slightly larger data set (a cross-section of about one hundred countries), this study is content to establish a statistically significant conditional correlation without seeking to make causal statements or addressing simultaneity. Their paper finds that federal systems are on average more corrupt. This result is shared by Kunicová and Rose-Ackerman (2005), who – in a paper that only tangentially focuses on the issue of our interest – use the World Bank Graft "Control Corruption" Index and TI's index as measures of corruption.

The most complete study in this strand of literature is the one by Fan, Lin, and Treisman (2009). They use a newly available data set of survey responses of businessmen and citizens about their concrete experiences with corruption. These measures are highly reliable as they relate to *personal* experiences of corruption; more importantly, they have been found to be only partially correlated with the other measures of corruption already mentioned, which are mainly based on expert opinions and perceptions. This survey is conducted in 80 countries in years 1999–2000, and specifically asks about personal experiences of bribe payments, their frequency, and amount. New data is also compiled on measuring decentralization, including number of tiers; average area of the lower tier; whether the constitution grants autonomy or sole responsibility of some service to subnational governments; and measures on whether the lower-tier politicians are directly elected by voters, indirectly chosen by local assemblies, or appointed from above. Their basic regression correlates the corruption variable with a battery of firm- and country-level variables, and of course variables related to fiscal decentralization. Their findings are very rich. First of all, having more tiers of government is correlated with higher levels of corruption. Decentralization, as measured by the share of subnational revenue, is strongly and *negatively* correlated with corruption. This is very interesting, especially given the more detailed and reliable data used in this paper, but it is heavily plagued by endogeneity, as fiscal decentralization may be more likely to be granted where corruption is known to be lower. There is also some evidence that civil service decentralization – measured by the share of civil servants employed by lower-tier units – is correlated with higher levels of corruption. These findings seem highly coherent with the theory: it is *fiscal* rather than administrative or political decentralization which may enhance accountability; similarly, constitutional arrangements, local spending, and employment per se are not helpful. The multiplication of decision units and of political intermediation, as proxied by the number and diffusion of local government tiers, appears to be positively correlated with the levels of corruption. The direction of causality is not explored in this work, but this paper is still able to convey a richer story on the link between decentralization and corruption.

Lessman and Markwardt (2010) take a long-run approach to the problem and compile a cross-section data set of 64 countries, including a long-run average of a measure of decentralization and corruption from the late nineties. This time mismatch is constructed to alleviate reverse causality and endogeneity problems, which is complemented by instrumenting decentralization with the log of the area of each country. For decentralization, they use both "de jure" measurements (federal constitutions, number of tiers) and "de facto" measures (local government revenues and expenditures and share of local government employment within the civil service). As corruption measures, ICRC and TI indices are both used, together with other similar measures for robustness. They also include a Freedom House index of freedom of the press and radio and newspaper penetration data. First and foremost, this study finds no significant link between decentralization and corruption. The lag structure and slightly larger size of the data set are indicated by the authors as the reason for this result, which is strikingly different from papers such as Fisman and Gatti (2002). Adding measures of freedom of the press and media penetration sheds some light on these results it appears that (de facto) decentralization has a positive effect – decreasing corruption – as long as there is sufficient freedom of the press and negative for those countries with lower freedom of the press. This paper highlights something that was already evident looking at micro-level evidence such as Ferraz and Finan (2008): decentralization per se may help accountability by bringing expenditure and taxation decisions closer to citizens, but this only works if voters have enough information to hold politicians accountable.

In a mainly theoretical paper, Albornoz and Cabrales (2013) construct a 110-country panel with data on corruption (from Transparency International, but also other measures as robustness check) and decentralization, for which they follow the same measures as in Fan, Lin, and Treisman (2009). Their main focus is to establish the joint effect of decentralization and political competition, measured with World Bank Voice and Accountability indicators. These are measurements of freedom of media and association aimed at capturing the citizens' involvement in selecting their government. They find that decentralization is linked with higher level of perceived corruption, but that this result disappears as political competition increases.

Ligthart and van Oudheusden (2015) use a different kind of data with respect to the ones just discussed, but address a cognate issue: decentralization may ease the control that citizens may exercise on public good provision; this is especially true when there are lively media players ready to uncover scandals and convey information, and when local spending is closely related to the revenue collected locally. If this is the case, we may expect that increased fiscal decentralization may enhance citizens' trust in the local government. They use data from three waves of World Value Survey (from 1994 to 2007), encompassing 42 countries. Using country-level averages, they find a statistically significant relationship between fiscal decentralization and trust in local government. These results are confirmed by individual-level regression, which also control for other variables detecting each individual trust for other people or institutions. The concern for reverse causality is obviously very strong: fiscal decentralization may be implemented in polities where local government is more trustworthy. These concerns are addressed instrumenting fiscal decentralization with lagged values of it, or by introducing country fixed effect. The latter, in particular, reduces the significance of the results. The authors of the study do everything possible to address endogeneity and reverse causality, but with so little within-country variation in fiscal decentralization measures, such a small number of countries in the sample, and the lack of a convincing instrument for fiscal decentralization, these results are difficult to interpret in a causal way.

All in all, these contributions mainly show the problems that arise when addressing a difficult question such as the structural link between decentralization and government accountability (and corruption in particular). Some regularities can be highlighted, though: first, de jure decentralization does not seem to have a robust effect on corruption, as it hides a wide array of de facto

References

Agrawal, D. (2014). LOST in America: Evidence on local sales taxes from national panel data. *Regional Science and Urban Economics*, **49**, 147–163.

Agrawal, D. (2015). The tax gradient: Spatial aspects of fiscal competition. *American Economic Journal: Economic Policy*, **7**, 1–30.

Agrawal, D. (2016). Local fiscal competition: An application to sales taxation with multiple federations. *Journal of Urban Economics*, **91**, 122–138.

Agrawal, D. & Foremny, D. (2019). Relocation of the rich: Migration in response to top tax rate changes from Spanish reforms. *Review of Economics and Statistics*, **101**, 214–232.

Albornoz, F. & Cabrales, A. (2013). Decentralization, political competition and corruption. *Journal of Development Economics*, **105**, 103–111.

Allain-Dupré, D. (2018). Assigning responsibilities across levels of government. OECD Working Papers on Fiscal Federalism, No. 24.

Allers, M. & Vermeulen, W. (2016). Capitalization of equalizing grants and the flypaper effect. *Regional Science and Urban Economics*, **58**, 115–129.

Alm, J. & Sheffrin, S. (2017). Using behavioral economics in public economics. *Public Finance Review*, **45**, 4–9.

Alt, J., Bueno de Mesquita, E. & Rose, S. (2011). Disentangling accountability and competence in elections: Evidence from U.S. term limits. *Journal of Politics*, **73**, 171–186.

Alt, J. E., Dryer-Lassen, D. & Rose, S. (2006). The causes of fiscal transparency: Evidence from the U.S. states. *IMF Staff Papers*, **53**, 30–57.

Alt, J. E., Dryer-Lassen, D. & Skilling, D. (2002). Fiscal transparency, gubernatorial approval, and the scale of government: Evidence from the states. *State Politics & Policy Quarterly*, **2**, 230–250.

Andersen, J., Fiva, J. & Natvik, G. (2014). Voting when the stakes are high. *Journal of Public Economics*, **110**, 157–166.

Aragón, F. (2013). Local spending, transfers, and costly tax collection. *National Tax Journal*, **66**, 343–370.

Aragón, F. & Pique, R. (2020) Better the devil you know? Reelected politicians and policy outcomes under no term limits. *Public Choice*, **182**, 1–16.

Banzhaf, H. & Walsh, R. (2008). Do people vote with their feet? An empirical test of Tiebout's mechanism. *American Economic Review*, **98**, 843–863.

Bardhan, P. & Mookherjee, D. (2000). Capture and Governance at Local and National Levels. *American Economic Reivew*, **90**, 135–139.

Barro, R. & Redlick, C. (2011). Macroeconomic effects from government purchases and taxes. *Quarterly Journal of Economics*, **126**, 51–102.

Bartik, T. (1985). Business location decisions in the United States: Estimates of the effects of unionization, taxes, and other characteristics of states. *Journal of Business & Economic Statistics*, **3**, 14–22.

Baskaran, T. (2012). Soft budget constraints and strategic interactions in subnational borrowing: Evidence from the German States, 1975–2005. *Journal of Urban Economics*, **71**, 114–127.

Baskaran, T. (2014). Identifying local tax mimicking with administrative borders and policy reform. *Journal of Public Economics*, **118**, 41–51.

Baskaran, T., Feld, L. & Schnellenbach, J. (2016). Fiscal federalism, decentralization, and economic growth: A meta-analysis. *Economic Inquiry*, **54**, 1445–1463.

Basten, C., Ehrlich, M. & Lassmann, A. (2017). Income taxes, sorting, and the costs of housing: Evidence from municipal boundaries in Switzerland. *Economic Journal*, **127**, 653–687.

Becker, E. (1996). The illusion of fiscal illusion: Unsticking the flypaper effect. *Public Choice*, **86**, 85–102.

Becker, J., Hopp, D. & Kriebel, M. (2020). Mental accounting of public funds: The flypaper effect in the lab. *Journal of Economic Behavior & Organization*, **176**, 321–326.

Belotti, F., Di Porto, E. & Santoni, G. (2016). The effect of local taxes on firm performance: Evidence from geo-referenced data. Working Paper No. 3/2016, Uppsala University, Department of Economics.

Ben-Bassat, A., Dahan, M. & Klor, E. F. (2016). Is centralization a solution to the soft budget constraint problem? *European Journal of Political Economy*, **45**, 57–75.

Besley, T. & Burgess, R. (2002). The Political Economy of Government Responsiveness: Theory and Evidence from India. *The Quarterly Journal of Economics*, **117**, 1415–1451.

Besley T. & Case, A. (1995a). Does electoral accountability affect economic policy choices? Evidence from gubernatorial term limits. *Quarterly Journal of Economics*, **110**, 769–798.

Besley T. & Case, A. (1995b). Incumbent behavior: Vote-seeking, tax-setting, and yardstick competition. *American Economic Review*, **85**, 25–45.

Besley, T. & Rosen, H. (1998). Vertical externalities in tax setting: Evidence from gasoline and cigarettes. *Journal of Public Economics*, **70**, 383–398.

Boadway, R. (2015). Intergovernmental transfers: Rationale and policy. In E. Ahmad & G. Brosio, eds., *Handbook of Multi-level Finance*. Cheltenham: Edward Elgar, pp. 410–436.

Boadway, R. & Flatters, F. (1982). Efficiency and equalization payments in a federal system of government: A synthesis and extension of recent results. *Canadian Journal of Economics*, **15**, 613–633.

Boadway, R. & Keen, M. (1996). Efficiency and the optimal direction of federal-state transfers. *International Tax and Public Finance*, **3**, 137–155.

Bordignon, M., Gamalerio, M. & Turati, G. (2013). Decentralization, vertical fiscal imbalance, and political selection. CESifo Working Paper 4459.

Bordignon, M., Grembi, V. & Piazza, S. (2017). Who do you blame in local finance? An analysis of municipal financing in Italy. *European Journal of Political Economy*, **49**, 146–163.

Bordignon, M. & Turati, G. (2009). Bailing out expectations and public health expenditure. *Journal of Health Economics*, **28**, 305–321.

Bracco, E., Lockwood, B., Porcelli, F. & Redoano, M. (2015). Intergovernmnetal grants as signals and the alignment effect: Theory and evidence. *Journal of Public Economics*, **123**, 78–91.

Breuillé, M-L. & Le Gallo, J. (2017). Spatial fiscal interactions among French municipalities within intermunicipal groups. *Applied Economics*, **49**, 4617–4637.

Brooks, L. & Phillips, J. (2010). An institutional explanation for the stickiness of federal grants. *Journal of Law, Economics and Organization*, **26**, 243–264.

Brueckner, J. (2003). Strategic interaction among governments: An overview of empirical studies. *International Regional Science Review*, **26**, 175–188.

Brulhart, M., Bucovetsky, S. & Schmidheiny, K. (2015). Taxes in cities: Interdependence, asymmetry and agglomeration. In G. Duranton, J. Vernon Henderson & W. Strange, eds., *Handbook of Regional and Urban Economics*. Amsterdam: Elsevier, pp. 1123–1196.

Brulhart, M. & Jametti, M. (2006). Vertical versus horizontal tax externalities: An empirical test. *Journal of Public Economics*, **90**, 2027–2062.

Brulhart, M., Jametti, M. & Schmidheiny, K. (2012). Do agglomeration economies reduce the sensitivity of firm location to tax differentials? *Economic Journal*, **122**, 1069–1093.

Brulhart, M. & Parchet, R. (2014). Alleged tax competition: The mysterious death of bequest taxes in Switzerland. *Journal of Public Economics*, **111**, 63–78.

Bucovetsky, S. & Smart, M. (2006). The efficiency consequences of local revenue equalization: Tax competition and tax distortions. *Journal of Public Economic Theory*, **8**, 119–144.

Buettner, T. (2006). The incentive effect of fiscal equalization transfers on tax policy. *Journal of Public Economics*, **90**, 477–497.

Buettner, T. & von Schwerin, A. (2016). Yardstick competition and partial coordination: Exploring the empirical distribution of local business tax rates. *Journal of Economic Behavior & Organization*, **124**, 178–201.

Cassette, A., Di Porto, E. & Foremny, D. (2012). Strategic fiscal interaction across borders: Evidence from French and German local governments across the Rhine Valley. *Journal of Urban Economics*, **72**, 17–30.

Calonico, S., Cattaneo, M., Farrell, M. H. & Titiunik, R. (2019). Regression Discontinuity Designs Using Covariates. *The Review of Economics and Statistics*, **101**, 442–451.

Chirinko, R. & Wilson, D. (2008). State investment tax incentives: A zero-sum game? *Journal of Public Economics*, **92**, 2362–2384.

Chirinko, R. & Wilson, D. (2017). Tax competition among US states: racing to the bottom or riding on a seesaw. *Journal of Public Economics*, **155**, 147–163.

Cloyne, J. (2013). Discretionary tax changes and the macroeconomy: New narrative evidence from the United Kingdom. *American Economic Review*, **103**, 1507–1528.

Costas-Pérez, E., Solé-Ollé, A. & Sorribas-Navarro, P. (2012). Corruption scandals, voter information, and accountability. *European Journal of Political Economy*, **28**, 469–484.

Coviello, D. & Gagliarducci, S. (2017). Tenure in office and public procurement. *American Economic Journal: Economic Policy*, **9**, 59–105.

Crivelli, E., Leive, A. & Stratmann, T. (2010). Subnational health spending and soft budget constraints in OECD countries. IMF Working Papers 10/147, International Monetary Fund.

Dahlberg, M., Mörk, E., Rattsø, J. & Ågren, H. (2008). Using a discontinuous grant rule to identify the effect of grants on local taxes and spending. *Journal of Public Economics*, **92**, 2320–2335.

Dahlby, B. (2011). The marginal cost of public funds and the flypaper effect. *International Tax and Public Finance*, **18**, 304–321.

Dahlby, B. & Ferede, E. (2016). The stimulative effect of intergovernmental grants and the marginal cost of public funds. *International Tax and Public Finance*, **23**, 114–139.

De Janvy, A., Finan, F. & Sadoulet, E. (2012). Local electoral incentives and decentralized program performance. *Review of Economics and Statistics*, **94**, 672–685.

Delgado, F., Lago-Penas, S. & Mayor, M. (2018). Local tax interaction and endogenous spatial weights basewd on quality of life. *Spatial Economic Analysis*, **13**, 296–318.

Devereux, M.P., Griffith, R. & Simpson, H. (2007). Firm location decisions, regional grants and agglomeration externalities. *Journal of Public Economics*, **91**, 413–435.

Dietrichson, J. & Ellegård, L. M. (2015). Assist or desist? Conditional bailouts and fiscal discipline in local governments. *European Journal of Political Economy*, **38**, 153–168.

Di Porto E. & Revelli, F. (2013). Tax limited reaction functions. *Journal of Applied Econometrics*, **28**, 823–839.

Dupor, B. (2017). So, why didn't the 2009 recovery act improve the nation's highways and bridges? *Federal Reserve Bank of St. Louis Review*, **99**, 169–182.

Duranton, J., Gobillon, L. & Overman, H. (2011). Assessing the effects of local taxation using microgeographic data. *Economic Journal*, **121**, 1017–1046.

Eugster, B. & Parchet, R. (2019). Culture and taxes. *Journal of Political Economy*, **127**, 296–337.

Fan, C.S., Lin, C. & Treisman, D. (2009). Political decentralization and corruption: Evidence from around the world. *Journal of Public Economics*, **93**, 14–34.

Fernández-Vázquez, P., Barberá, P. & Rivero, G. (2016). Rooting out corruption or rooting for corruption? The heterogeneous electoral consequences of scandals. *Political Science Research and Methods*, **4**, 379–397.

Ferraz, C. & Finan, F. (2008). Exposing corrupt politicians: The effects of Brazil's publicly released audits on electoral outcomes. *Quarterly Journal of Economics*, **123**, 703–745.

Fisman, R. & Gatti, R. (2002). Decentralization and corruption: Evidence across countries. *Journal of Public Economics*, **83**, 325–345.

Freret. S. & Maguain, D. (2017). The effects of agglomeration on tax competition: Evidence from a two-regime spatial panel data model on French data. *International Tax and Public Finance*, **24**, 1100–1140.

Gamkhar, S. & Oates, W. (1996). Asymmetries in the response to increases and decreases intergovernmental grants: some empirical findings. *National Tax Journal*, **49**, 501–512.

Gamkhar, S. & Shah, A. (2007). The impact of intergovernmental transfers: A synthesis of the conceptual and empirical literature. In R. Boadway & A. Shah, eds., *Intergovernmental Fiscal Transfers: Principles and Practice*. Washington, DC: World Bank, pp. 225–258.

Gennari, E. & Messina, G. (2014). How sticky are local expenditures in Italy? Assessing the relevance of the flypaper effect through municipal data. *International Tax and Public Finance*, **21**, 324–344.

Gerring, J. & Thaker, S. (2004). Political institutions and corruption: The role of unitarism and parliamentarism. *British Journal of Political Science*, **34**, 295–330.

Geys, B., Heinemann, F. & Kalb, A. (2010). Voter involvement, fiscal autonomy and public sector efficiency: Evidence from German municipalities. *European Journal of Political Economy*, **26**, 265–278.

Gibbons S. & Overman H. (2012). Mostly pointless spatial econometrics? *Journal of Regional Science* **52**, 172–191.

Goeminne, S., Smolders, C. & Vandorpe, E. (2017). The real impact of a one-off fiscal restriction: empirical evidence of a flypaper effect in Flemish municipalities. *Public Money & Management*, **37**, 285–292.

Gonçalves, S. (2014). The effects of participatory budgeting on municipal expenditures and infant mortality in Brazil. *World Development*, **53**, 94–110.

Goodspeed, T. (2000). Tax structure in a federation. *Journal of Public Economics*, **75**, 493–506.

Gordon, N. (2004). Do federal grants boost school spending? Evidence from Title I. *Journal of Public Economics*, **88**, 1771–1792.

Greenhalgh-Stanley, N., Rohlin, S. & Thompson, J. (2018). Food sales taxes and employment. *Journal of Regional Science*, **58**, 1003–1016.

Hamilton, J. (1986). The flypaper effect and the deadweight loss from taxation. *Journal of Urban Economics*, **19**, 148–155.

Harger, K. & Ross, A. (2016). Do capital tax incentives attract new businesses? Evidence across industries from the new markets tax credit. *Journal of Regional Science*, **56**, 733–753.

Hilber, C. (2011). The economic implications of house price capitalization: A survey of an emerging literature. SERC Discussion Paper No. 0091, Spatial Economics Research Centre, LSE.

Hines, J. & Thaler, R. (1995). Anomalies. The flypaper effect. *Journal of Economic Perspectives*, **9**, 217–226.

Holmes, T. (1998). The effect of state policies on the location of manufacturing: Evidence from state borders. *Journal of Political Economy*, **106**, 667–705.

Inman, R. (2009). Flypaper effect. In S. Durlauf & L. Blume, eds., *The New Palgrave Dictionary of Economics Online*. London: Palgrave Macmillan, pp. 1–6.

Isen, A. (2014). Do local government fiscal spillovers exist? Evidence from counties, municipalities, and school districts. *Journal of Public Economics*, **110**, 57–73.

Ivanyna, M. & Shah, A. (2014). How close is your government to its people? Worldwide indicators on localization and decentralization. *Economics: The Open-Access, Open-Assessment E-Journal*, **8**, 1–61.

Keen, M. (1998). Vertical tax externalities in the theory of fiscal federalism. *IMF Staff Papers*, **45**, 454–485.

Klašnja, M. (2015). Corruption and the incumbency disadvantage: Theory and evidence. *Journal of Politics*, **77**, 928–942.

Klašnja, M. & Titiunik, R. (2017). The incumbency curse: Weak parties, term limits, and unfulfilled accountability. *American Political Science Review*, **111**, 129–148.

Klein, F. A. & Sakurai, S. N. (2015). Term limits and political budget cycles at the local level: evidence from a young democracy. *European Journal of Political Economy*, **37**, 21–36,

Kleven, H., Landais, C., Saez, E. & Schultz, E. (2014). Migration and wage effects of taxing top earners: Evidence from the foreigners' tax scheme in Denmark. *Quarterly Journal of Economics*, **129**, 333–378.

Knack, S. & Keefer, P. (1997). Does social capital have an economic payoff? A cross-country investigation. *Quarterly Journal of Economics*, **112**, 1251–1288.

Kuminoff, N., Smith, K. & Timmins, C. (2013). The new economics of equilibrium sorting and policy evaluation using housing markets. *Journal of Economic Literature*, **51**, 1007–1062.

Kunicová, J. & Rose-Ackerman, S. (2005). Electoral rules and constitutional structures as constraints on corruption. *British Journal of Political Science*, **35**, 573–606.

Knight, B. (2002). Endogenous federal grants and crowd-out of state government spending: Theory and evidence from the federal highway program. *American Economic Review*, **92**, 71–92.

Kornai, J. (1986). The soft budget constraint. *Kyklos*, **39**, 3–30.

Kornai, J., Maskin E. & Roland, G. (2003). Understanding the soft budget constraint. *Journal of Economic Literature*, **41**, 1095–1136.

Leduc, S. & Wilson, D. (2017). Are state governments roadblocks to federal stimulus? Evidence on the flypaper effect of highway grants in the 2009 Recovery Act. *American Economic Journal: Economic Policy*, **9**, 253–292.

Lessmann, C. & Markwardt, G. (2010). One size fits all? Decentralization, corruption, and the montoring of bureaucrats. *World Development*, **38**, 631–646.

Liebig, T., Puhani, P. & Sousa-Poza, A. (2007). Taxation and internal migration: Evidence from the Swiss census using community-level variation in income tax rates. *Journal of Regional Science*, **47**, 807–836.

Liebig, T. & Sousa-Poza, A. (2006). The influence of taxes on migration: Evidence from Switzerland. *Cambridge Journal of Economics*, **30**, 235–252.

Ligthart, J. & van Oudheusden, P. (2015). In government we trust: The role of fiscal decentralization. *European Journal of Political Economy*, **37**, 116–128.

Litschig, S. & Morrison, K. (2013). The impact of intergovernmental transfers on education outcomes and poverty reduction. *American Economic Journal: Applied Economics*, **5**, 206–240.

Liu, C. & Ma, G. (2016). Taxation without representation: Local fiscal response to intergovernmental transfers in China. *International Tax and Public Finance*, **23**, 854–874.

Liu, Y. & Martinez-Vazquez, J. (2014). Interjurisdictional tax competition in China. *Journal of Regional Science*, **54**, 606–628.

Lowry, R., Alt, J. & Ferree, K. (1998). Fiscal policy outcomes and electoral accountability in American states. *American Political Science Review*, **92**, 759–774.

Lundquist, H. (2015). Granting public or private consumption? Effects of grants on local public spending and income taxes. *International Tax and Public Finance*, **22**, 41–72.

Lutz, B. (2010). Taxation with representation: Intergovernmental grants in a plebiscite democracy. *Review of Economics and Statistics*, **92**, 316–332.

Lyytikainen, T. (2012). Tax competition among local governments: Evidence from a property tax reform in Finland. *Journal of Public Economics*, **96**, 584–595.

Manski, C. (1993). Identification of endogenous social effects: The reflection problem. *Review of Economic Studies*, **60**, 531–542.

Martinez, I. (2017). Beggar-thy-neighbor tax cuts: Mobility after a local income and wealth tax reform in Switzerland. Working Paper LISER No. 08.

Maskin, E. S. (1999). Recent theoretical work on the soft budget constraint. *American Economic Review*, **89**, 421–425.

Milligan, K. & Smart. M. (2019). An estimable model of income redistribution in a federation: Musgrave meets Oates. *American Economic Journal: Economic Policy*, **11**, 406–434.

Moretti, E. & Wilson, D. (2017). The effect of state taxes on the geographical location of top earners: Evidence from star scientists. *American Economic Review*, **107**, 1859–1903.

Nesbit, T. & Kreft, S. (2009). Federal grants, earmarked revenues, and budget crowd-out: State highway funding. *Public Budgeting & Finance*, **29**, 94–110.

Oates, W. (1972). *Fiscal Federalism*. New York: Harcourt Brace Jovanovich.

OECD/UCLG (2016). *Subnational Governments around the World: Structure and Finance*. Paris: OECD.

Parchet, R. (2019). Are local tax rates strategic complements or strategic substitutes? *American Economic Journal: Economic Policy*, **11**, 189–224.

Perez-Sebastian, F. & Raveh, O. (2018). What drives vertical fiscal interactions? Evidence from the 1980 crude oil windfall act, *Regional Science and Urban Economics*, **73**, 251–268.

Pettersson-Lidbom, P. (2010). Dynamic commitment and the soft budget constraint: An empirical test. *American Economic Journal: Economic Policy*, **2**, 154–179.

Prud'homme, R. (1995). The dangers of decentralization. *The World Bank Research Observer*, **10**, 201–220.

Putnam, R. (1993). *Making Democracy Work: Civic Traditions in Modern Italy*. Princeton: Princeton University Press.

Rathelot, R. & Sillard, P. (2008). The importance of local corporate taxes in business location decisions: Evidence from French micro data. *Economic Journal*, **118**, 499–514.

Reigenwertz, Y. (2018). Corporate taxes and vertical tax externalities: Evidence from narrative federal shocks. *Regional Science and Urban Economics*, **68**, 84–97.

Revelli, F. (2006). Spatial interactions among governments. In E. Ahmad & G. Brosio, eds., *Handbook of Fiscal Federalism*. Cheltenham: Edward Elgar, pp. 106–130.

Revelli, F. (2013). Tax mix corners and other kinks. *Journal of Law and Economics*, **56**, 741–776.

Revelli, F. (2015a). Geografiscal federalism. In E. Ahmad & G. Brosio, eds., *Handbook of Multilevel Finance*. Cheltenham: Edward Elgar, pp. 107–123.

Revelli, F. (2015b). Tax mandates and factor input use: Theory and evidence from Italy. *FinanzArchiv: Public Finance Analysis*, **71**, 328–359.

Revelli, F. (2016a). Tax limits and local elections. *Public Choice*, **166**, 53–68.

Revelli, F. (2016b). A comparative view of local tax and expenditure limitations and their consequences. In: T. Eisenberg & G. Ramello, eds., *Comparative Law and Economics*. Cheltenham: Edward Elgar, pp. 161–181.

Reynolds, C. & Rohlin, S. (2014). Do location-based tax incentives improve quality of life and quality of business environment? *Journal of Regional Science*, **54**, 1–32.

Reynolds, C. & Rohlin, S. (2015). The effects of location-based tax policies on the distribution of household income: Evidence from the federal Empowerment Zone program. *Journal of Urban Economics*, 88, 1–15.

Rhode, P. & Strumpf, K. (2003). Assessing the importance of Tiebout sorting: Local heterogeneity from 1850 to 1990. *American Economic Review*, **93**, 1648–1677.

Rohlin, S. & Thompson, J. (2018). Local sales taxes, employment, and tax competition. *Regional Science and Urban Economics*, **70**, 373–383.

Romer, D. & Romer, H. (2010). The macroeconomic effects of tax changes: Estimates based on a new measure of fiscal shocks. *American Economic Review*, **100**, 763–801.

Ryu, J. (2017). Measuring the flypaper effect: The interaction between lump-sum aid and the substitution effect of matching aid. *Public Finance and Management*, **17**, 48–70.

Seabright, P. (1996). Accountability and decentralisation in government: An incomplete contracts model. *European Economic Review*, **40**, 61–89.

Shleifer A. & Vishny R.W. (1993). Corruption. NBER Working Papers 4372.

Schmidheiny, K. (2006). Income segregation and local progressive taxation: Empirical evidence from Switzerland. *Journal of Public Economics*, **90**, 429–458.

Schmidheiny, K. & Slotwinski, M. (2018). Behavioral responses to local tax rates: Quasi-experimental evidence from a foreigners' tax scheme in Switzerland. *Journal of Public Economics*, **167**, 293–324.

Smart, M. (2007). The incentive effects of grants. In R. Boadway & A. Shah, eds., *Intergovernmental Fiscal Transfers: Principles and Practice*. Washington, DC: The World Bank, pp. 203–223.

Sorens, J. (2016). Vertical fiscal gaps and economic performance: A theoretical review and empirical meta-analysis. Mercatus Working Paper, Mercatus Center at George Mason University, February.

Sorribas-Navarro, P. (2011). Bailouts in a fiscal federal system: Evidence from Spain. *European Journal of Political Economy*, **27**, 154–170.

Thaler, R. (1999). Mental accounting matters. *Journal of Behavioral Decision Making*, **12**, 183–206.

Tiebout, C. (1956). A pure theory of local expenditures. *Journal of Political Economy*, **64**, 416–424.

Treisman, D. (2000). The causes of corruption: a cross-national study. *Journal of Public Economics*, **76**, 399–457.

Vegh, C. & Vuletin, G. (2015). Unsticking the flypaper effect in an uncertain world. *Journal of Public Economics*, **131**, 142–155.

Vegh, C. & Vuletin, G. (2016). Unsticking the flypaper effect using distortionary taxation. *Económica*, **LXII**, 185–237.

Wang, J. (2018) Strategic interaction and economic development incentives policy: Evidence from U.S. states. *Regional Science and Urban Economics*, **68**, 249–259.

Weingast, B. R. (1995). The economic role of political institutions: Market-preserving federalism and economic development. *Journal of Law, Economics, and Organization*, **11**, 1–31.

Wildasin, D. E. (1997). Externalities and bailouts: hard and soft budget constraints in intergovernmental fiscal relations. Policy Research Working Paper Series 1843, World Bank.

Young, C. & Varner, C. (2011). Millionaire migration and state taxation of top incomes: Evidence from a natural experiment. *National Tax Journal*, **64**, 255–283.

Young, C., Varner, C., Lurier, I. & Prisinzano, R. (2016). Millionaire migration and taxation of the elite: Evidence from administrative data. *American Sociological Review*, **81**, 421–446.